BARBECUE GREATS
MEMPHIS STYLE

BARBECUE GREATS
MEMPHIS STYLE

GREAT RESTAURANTS
GREAT RECIPES
GREAT PERSONALITIES

BY CAROLYN WELLS

PIG OUT PUBLICATIONS

Cover photo: Courtesy of the National Pork Producers Council
Cover design: Jim Langford

ISBN 0-925175-03-X

Printed in the United States of America

10   9   8   7   6   5   4   3   92   93   94

CONTENTS

CONTENTS

CONTENTS

CONTENTS

ACKNOWLEDGMENTS

This book is the result of the combined efforts of many fellow barbecue enthusiasts. Barbecuers are just plain nice folks. Their support and enthusiasm took this concept from dream to reality. We ate a lot of 'Que and had a lot of fun on the way.

Acknowledgment and thanks go to my husband, Gary Wells, for believing in me and in this venture; to my co-publisher, Karen Adler, for sharing the dream and research; and to the editor and production co-ordinator, Jane Guthrie, for getting the book to print.

Thanks also go to Ida Eleazer; Carolyn Guckert and the other Memphis in May folks; to Bill, John, and Janie Thompson of the Paddlewheel Porkers, who acted as a sounding board; to Ardie Davis, Paul Kirk, and Bruce Daniel for their input and advice; and to Wynne and Eloise Bellerjeau, Rita Roberson, Tammy Williams, Greg Johnson, and Vince Staten for their support and encouragement.

And to the pitmasters who gave so freely of their recipes and cooking techniques: Jim Quessenberry, Jerry Roach, Tom Sampson, Tex Caviness, Jim Turner, Joellyn Forrester, Lil Hamrick, Ed and Sonny Daniel, Ernie Freeland, Rick Cooper, Alex Camacho, Charles Custer, Red Gill, Darrell Hicks, Matt Fisher, Senator Jim Sasser, Larry Thomason, Linda Thomason, Billy "Shug" Powell, Jim Avent, Silky Sullivan, Jim Marty, John Willingham, Chuck Slaten, Jim and Sherril Blair, Chris Gang, Jim Ward, and Bubba and Beverly Norris.

And to the restauranteurs who served up great Memphis barbecue while we were researching the book.

Last, but by no means least, thanks to the National Pork Producers Council for their assistance and for the cover photo.

INTRODUCTION

Barbecue has been a part of the Memphis culture as long as anyone can remember. A phenomenon called the Memphis in May International Barbecue Cooking Contest grew out of an obsession with slow smoked, lovingly tended, well-seasoned ribs, shoulders, and whole hog.

The Memphis in May International Barbecue Cooking Contest is held the third weekend in May at Tom Lee Park, which overlooks the mighty Mississippi River. The event attracts 176 teams, 140 of which are from the mid-South. These teams spend untold hours honing their barbecuing skills and concocting secret sauces. You see fancy rigs, basted pigs, outrageous costumes, porcine puns, stickers on buns, stickers on bosoms, entertainment from a huge stage and from team booths—all of which is accented by the sweet smell of hickory smoke, a smiling Mississippi River, and a sky painted mid-South blue. Here barbecue bravado, bragging, competition, and celebration reach their zenith! Here you will find the most bodacious, flowery, earthy, arrogant descriptions of barbecue on earth. You'll find a sense of community and a celebration unequaled. You'll eat some of the best barbecue you've ever tasted. And you'll bask in an inimitable combination of good people, good times, and good food.

The teams who compete in Memphis in May and affiliated contests are serious about their barbecue and just as serious about having a good time. Exemplars of true Southern hospitality, they have generously provided us with great barbecue recipes and cooking techniques. In the Memphis barbecue tradition, pork is the most often featured meat. However, recipes for beef, lamb, poultry, fish/seafood, and wild game are also included. Tantalizing sauces, rubs, and marinades enhance the flavor of these entrees, and delicious accompaniments complete the menu. The selected team biographies interspersed throughout the recipes will introduce you to the great barbecuers and the spirit with which they share their tips and techniques.

The only thing as good as cooking and eating Memphis-style barbecue at home, at a friend's house, or at a barbecue contest is eating at one of the eighty or so restaurants in Memphis serving barbecue. If you polled twenty Memphians as to their favorite barbecue restaurant, you'd likely get twenty different answers. This is hog heaven; you can decide for yourself. We have included eleven restaurants to get you started on the odessey. And here's a plus—Memphis is world headquarters of Federal Express and world headquarters of Federal Expressed ribs. If you live outside Memphis, there are restaurants that will Federal Express complete barbecue meals to you.

So, begin your journey into the delights and depths of sassy sauces, spicy dry rubs, and marvelous marinades. Whether you're a novice at the "sport" or have been around the smoker a few times, welcome to world class barbecue—Memphis Style.

MEMPHIS IN MAY
WORLD CHAMPIONSHIP BARBECUE
COOKING CONTEST

The Memphis in May World Championship Barbecue Cooking Contest is a major event in the month-long Memphis in May Festival. First held in 1977 in a small vacant lot, it was conceived by a few creative young thinkers who recognized one simple fact: that Memphis was—hands down, no questions asked—the pork barbecue cooking capital of the world. The event was inspired by the region's appetite for pork barbecue—chopped or pulled, whole hog or shoulder, wet or dry—and its mysterious sauces—tangy, sweet, hot, thick, or thin. Encouraged by numerous serious backyard chefs and nurtured by their own "hog-wild" imaginations, the founders scraped together a few thousand dollars to produce the first contest on May 5, 1978.

Twenty teams competed that first year for $1,000 in prize money. The winner, Bessie Mae Cathey, attributed her success to "ribs that came from high on the hog." When asked how she knew that she cooked good barbecue, she said, "because everybody who eats it says it is." When the smoke cleared and the last of the barbecue bones had been sucked dry and the judges had washed down the spicy meat with kegs of Budweiser, Memphis in May knew it had a winner.

The next year the contest moved to Tom Lee Park, right on the banks of Ol' Man River, allowing more space for the region's backyard professionals and opening up some breathing room to party. And that space to cook and to party was apparently the most important ingredient in the event's recipe for success. Eleven years later, in 1988, the World Championship Barbecue Contest awarded $10,000 in prize money, accommodated 174 teams and turned down about 50, sanctioned forty contests across the U.S., used 175 judges in three categories (whole hog, shoulder, and ribs), featured Ms. Piggy, Hog Calling, Showmanship, and the Porker Promenade, and attracted 80,000 spectators.

Nearly thirty events currently comprise the Memphis in May sanctioned barbecue contest network. The following is a list of the calendar of events:

JANUARY Pine Castle Pig Fiesta in the Sun, Orlando, FL. *Contact:* Fred Burnett (407) 281-8353

MARCH

Louisiana State Barbecue Championship, Lafayette, LA. *Contact:* Nelson Schexnayder (318) 231-6193.

Ozark Hawg BBQ, Batesville, AR. *Contact:* Dr. Jim Stalker (501) 793-5205

March on McLean, Memphis, TN. *Contact:* Harold Lesher (901) 323-2627

APRIL

Razorback State Championship Barbecue Cook-Off, Blytheville, AR. *Contact:* Darrell McGee (501) 763-3881

Southaven Spring Festival Barbecue Contest, Southaven, MS. *Contact:* Gerald Wilson (601) 396-5727

MAY

Memphis in May World Championship Barbecue Cooking Contest, Memphis, TN. *Contact:* Memphis in May (901) 525-4611

Ohio River Arts Festival Barbecue Cooking Contest, Evansville, IN. *Contact:* Kim Setzer (812) 422-2111

JUNE

Delta Jubilee—Mississippi Championship Barbecue Cooking Contest, Clarksdale, MS. *Contact:* Maggie Monty (601) 627-7337

Lock 'n' Ham Jam, Augusta, GA. *Contact:* Beth Jones (404) 826-4702

Wynn Farm Fest, Wynn, AR. *Contact:* Eldridge Brawner (501) 238-3655

Winchester "High on the Hog" Barbecue Cookoff, Winchester, TN. *Contact:* Barbara Lamb (615) 967-7418

Arkansas State Bar-B-Q Championship, Little Rock, AR. *Contact:* Bill Walker (501) 224-9158

Lakeland Civic Club Annual Funfest, Lakeland, TN. *Contact:* Tom Jenkins (901) 682-2777

W. C. Handy Blues and BBQ Festival, Henderson, KY. *Contact:* Malcolm Neel (502) 827-1577

JUNE (*cont.*)

Dyersburg, TN. *Contact:* Eddy Gregory (901) 286-1500

Show-Me State Championship Barbecue Cook-Off, Kennett, MO. *Contact:* J. R. Blackburn (314) 888-4571

High on the Mississippi Hog Cooking Contest, Greenwood, MS. *Contact:* Larry Young (601) 455-6397

JULY

Hog Wild in July, Jackson, MS. *Contact:* Doug McCurley (601) 354-3006

Covington Jaycees BBQ Cooking Contest, Covington, TN. *Contact:* John Walker (901) 476-4932

DuQuoin State Barbecue Cookoff, DuQuoin, IL. *Contact:* Angela Roach (618) 542-8338

AUGUST

Meat on the Mississippi, Carruthersville, MO. *Contact:* Judge Luber (314) 333-2797

Yazoo Hawg Day Afternoon, Yazoo City, MS. *Contact:* Sandra Ragland (601) 746-1273

Mid-Continent Truck Stop Barbecue, Brownsville, TN. *Contact:* Ronnie Jones (901) 772-3444

SEPTEMBER

Murphysboro Barbecue Championship, Murphysboro, IL. *Contact:* Mike Mills (618) 684-2775

Possum Town Pig Fest—Mississippi State Championship, Columbus, MS. *Contact:* Bubba Norris (601) 328-4532

OCTOBER

Riverfeast, Knoxville, TN. *Contact:* Chip Scott (615) 523-7543

Hog Wild in Corinth, Corinth, MS. *Contact:* Ella Jean Whalen (601) 287-5269

OCTOBER (cont.) Russellville Pork Roast, Russellville, AR. *Contact:* Troy Burris (501) 968-4888

Cleveland October Fest Barbecue Cook-Off, Cleveland, MS. *Contact:* Demetra Myers (601) 843-2712

The Big Pig Jig, Vienna, GA. *Contact:* Judy Ledford (912) 268-4744

Arkansas Invitational Barbecue Championship, West Memphis, AR. *Contact:* Keith Harlow (501) 732-6085

Cityfest Barbecue Cooking Contest, Tuscaloosa, AL. *Contact:* Gene Poole (205) 752-5535

NOVEMBER First Coast Ham Jam, Orange Park, FL. *Contact:* Kim Brown (904) 264-2651

Bamberg County Oink Feast, Denmark, SC. *Contact:* W. Alfred Matheny (803) 793-4963

DECEMBER Christmas on the River Barbecue Cooking Contest, Demopolis, AL. *Contact:* George Franks (205) 289-5459

For further information, contact Memphis in May at (901) 525-4611.

BARBECUE BASICS

GRILLING AND BARBECUING: TWO DIFFERENT THINGS

Many people have notions about outdoor cooking that lead them astray. "Let's have barbecue," your host says, as he proceeds to torch an unsuspecting chicken over an open flame, two inches above white-hot coals. Seriously, it doesn't take a Ph.B. to appreciate the not-too-subtle difference between barbecuing and grilling. When *grilling,* the fire's hot. Meats cook rapidly over direct heat to maximize juice rentention and seal in moisture. *Barbecuing* is slow cooking at a relatively low temperature (180 to 300 degrees) over direct or indirect heat. Both methods, of course, have merit. Grilling or barbecuing/smoking, the basic equipment is essentially the same. A covered unit makes the most sense because it can be used for both types of cooking.

THE EQUIPMENT

Open brazier. This unit is a shallow container with a grid on which to put what you're cooking (like a hibachi); it is suitable only for grilling.

Covered cooker. This encompasses almost everything else. These cookers come in all shapes and sizes, from Weber-type "kettles" to rectangular units. They serve for both grilling and barbecuing. To use for barbecuing, the unit must have vents for proper ventilation and temperature control.

Japanese kamado. This a a ceramic "egg-shaped" cooker, with a firebox in the bottom and an adjustable air vent. The tight-fitting lid makes it an excellent smoker.

Water smoker. This dome-shaped cooker has a firebox in the bottom, water tray in the middle, and grid at the top. It's excellent for slow smoking with indirect heat.

Gas or electric grills. These cookers are easy to use and clean and are popular with weekend chefs. Primarily for grilling, they can be used to barbecue by keeping the heat very low and adding a water pan for moisture. Smoke flavor can be achieved by wrapping wood chips in heavy-duty aluminum foil, poking holes in the pack, and placing it directly on lava rock. When you're through cooking, discard the smoke chip packet. No mess, great smoke flavor.

55-gallon drum. These make great cookers. The book *Real Barbecue* (see "Books on Barbecue," p. 126) has instructions on building your own.

TOOLS AND ACCESSORIES

Meat thermometer. This is the most under-utilized utensil in barbecue cookery. Use it to measure the internal temperature of meat cuts to check for doneness.

Charcoal chimney. A clean, handy way to start charcoal. Load the chimney with charcoal and newspaper; start a fire with no petroleum or chemicals.

Tongs (two pairs). Use one for handling meats (never pierce meat with a fork). Use the other for moving or refueling hot coals.

Spray bottle of water. Keep one handy to extinguish flare-ups.

Heavy-duty glove, mitt, or hot pad. This is a must to protect your hands.

Basting brush, paint brush, or small cotton "mop." Any of these is great for basting.

Candy thermometer. Place one in the top grill vent to guage your cooking temperature.

Wire brush. This is the way to clean your grill.

Snazzy apron. How else will they know you're the Chief Chef?

THE FUEL

Use high quality hardwood charcoal briquettes or lump charcoal. The cheaper varieties sometimes have a great deal of coal added. Use a chimney starter; when the coals are ready, add them to the grill. Or, you can start the coals right in your grill. Make a mound of briquettes and douse them with charcoal starter before lighting (NEVER use gasoline). Allow briquettes to burn until they are 80% ashed over. Spread them out, replace the grill, and you're ready to cook.

Additional smoke flavor can be achieved by using wood chips or chunks. Most non-resinous woods work well. Chips and chunks can be soaked in water, then placed directly on the coals. Or wrap chips (wet or dry) in heavy-duty aluminum foil, poke holes in the top of the packet, and place it on the coals. Most people are familiar with barbecued foods smoked with hickory or mesquite, and these woods are widely available. However, fruitwoods are wonderful for smoking—apple, cherry, peach, pear. Grapevine adds a light delicate smoke to fish or chicken. Pecan, alder, sassafras, or persimmon also add flavor and aroma. It's okay to experiment; just don't use pine!

MOISTURE

Some barbecuers swear that a "water tray" is a necessary element of good barbecue cookery. Others never use one. Try it both ways and decide for yourself. The water tray/pan can be placed directly on the coals to make indirect heat, or it can be placed to the side of the grill. Either way, it imparts moisture in the cooking chamber.

RUBS, MARINADES, AND SAUCES

Barbecue cooking is a subjective experience. One of the most valuable parts of this book is its collection of sauces, rubs, and marinades. Many teams are devoted to particular brands. If a brand name is specified that's not available in your area, substitute your favorite (or check the "Mail Order" section at the back of this book). Be creative and use your favorite herbs and spices for recipe variations.

Rubs are blends of dry spices. Dry rubs are applied to the meat to tenderize and flavor it prior to cooking.

Marinades are liquid blends in which to soak meats prior to cooking. Some can also be used as bastes during the cooking process. Marinades contain spices, vinegar, wine, and/or other flavoring and tenderizing agents that are absorbed into the meat.

Sauces are usually tomato-based blends that can enhance barbecue. They should be used only during the final stages of cooking or served "on the side" as a condiment.

TIME

A grilled meal can be completed in relatively short order. But barbecuing "takes as long as it takes." Cooking times will vary with the type of cooking unit, the amount of fuel, and the size of the barbecue meat. So, relax and get out your handy meat thermometer. Follow the directions that come with it for use. Beef and lamb are rare at 130 degrees and well done at 160 degrees. Pork should be cooked to 170 degrees, and poultry to 165 degrees.

PORK

POT BELLIED PORKERS HOG

105-lb. hog, round dressed
1 lb. butter
vegetable oil
1/2 gal. Wicker's Marinade and Baste

WHOLE HOG SEASONING:

1/2 C. Italian seasoning
1/4 C. coarse ground black pepper
1/4 C. oregano
1/4 C. lemon pepper
1/2 C. minced garlic
1/4 C. thyme leaves
1/8 C. crushed red pepper

FINISHING SAUCE:

1 qt. Wicker's Marinade and Baste
1 qt. barbecue sauce
1 pt. red wine vinegar
1 (46 oz.) can V-8 juice

Trim hog of excess fat and rub body cavity with butter. Combine hog seasoning ingredients and sprinkle onto meat (use all of the seasoning).

Place hog on cooker back side up and cook for 5 hours, rubbing skin with oil every hour. Flip hog, add Wicker's sauce to cavity, and cook for 17 more hours at 225 degrees. Baste every hour. Prepare finishing sauce and apply to cooking meat 1 hour prior to serving.

Serves a small army

POUNDED PORK TENDERS

2 pork tenderloins
W'ham Mild or Cajun Hot Seasoning

Cut meat in 4 to 5 ounce portions, approximately 1/2-inch thick and 4 inches in diameter. Pound meat with a tenderizer mallet. Sprinkle liberally with W'ham seasoning. Let set 1 hour to overnight, depending on desired level of spiciness. Grill over hot coals until done, about 10 minutes each side.

Serves 4-6

FEDERAL EXPRESS PORKY PILOTS

The Porky Pilots team is made up entirely of Federal Express pilots and employees. Chief cook Jim Ward states, "To the best of my knowledge we are the most consistent placing team in the Whole Hog Division." At Memphis in May they won First Place in 1983 and placed in the top five in 1984, 1986, 1987, and 1988. At the Lakeland Barbecue Contest, they took First Place in 1987 and Third Place in 1988 in the Whole Hog Division.

One of the secrets to the Porky Pilots whole hog cooking success is their low temperature, slow cooking process. Jim relates this story passed on to him when he was an apprentice barbecuer: "Pork barbecue was first cooked in the mid-South by placing an old bedspring over a fire (the bedspring served as the grill). An old car hood was used as a cover to hold the smoke in. I asked an old timer what temperature was used, and he just laughed and said, 'We didn't have thermometers back then.' We keep a temperature as low as we can and just watch the flies. If the flies land on your meat, the fire is not hot enough."

Ever loyal, Jim forwarded recipes for this book via Federal Express—wish he'd sent some hog, too!

PORKY PILOTS WHOLE HOG

150-175 lb. hog, dressed
Table Sauce (*p. 81*)

BASTING SAUCE:

2-3 oz. paprika
1 lb. meat tenderizer
3 qt. oil

2 qt. vinegar
2-3 qt. water
6 celery stalks and tops,
   cut into 3 pieces
2 onions, sliced in rings
2 lemons, sliced in rings
2 (12 oz.) cans beer

To prepare basting sauce, sauté onions and celery pieces in an appropriate amount of oil. Add the remaining ingredients and heat. Set aside.

Prepare a bed of hot charcoal (100% hardwood) and then cover it with a blend of wet green persimmon and hickory sawdust. (The sawdust will steam and keep meat moist, it will smoke and give the meat flavor, and it will produce heat to cook the meat.) Repeat fueling process every hour.

Maintain temperature of 160-180 degrees and cook hog meat side down over direct heat for 5 hours, basting every hour. Turn the hog to the skin side down and cook at 180-200 degrees for 19 to 21 hours more, basting every half hour. One hour prior to serving, baste the hog with Table Sauce and let temperature drop so that Table Sauce does not burn.

When serving, pull the meat away from the bone with your hands. DO NOT use a knife to cut the meat away from the bone. If you have to cut barbecue from the bone, it's not barbecue and won't be fit to eat!

Serves a large army or air force

TWISTER RIBS

2 slabs baby loin back ribs (pound and a half and down)
Tail Twisters "Shake Sauce"

Skin ribs and trim as if you were serving them to an IRS auditor. Rub gently with sauce. Let ribs sit at room temperature for a minimum of 30 minutes or until moisture begins to draw. Cook over indirect heat with a little hickory smoke at 275 degrees for 3 1/2 to 4 hours, turning once an hour. (Fight off the temptation to look at ribs every 10 minutes—opening the cooker prolongs cooking time and plays havoc with keeping an even temperature.)

Serves 4-6

TAIL TWISTERS

The Tail Twisters team was created in 1986 and is made up of Larry and Diane Thomason and Kneibert and Janis Stillman. Both couples are from Kennett, Missouri. Larry and Kneibert cook, and Janice and Diane run everything else.

The team won the title of Show-Me State Champion at their very first contest and have earned at least a First Place in every contest they've entered except two. The Twisters have placed twice in the top ten in their category at Memphis in May. They use a dry seasoning in their cooking and have recently begun marketing their "Shake Sauce" by mail.

When he's not cooking in contests or mixing up his secret seasoning, Larry is a Missouri State Representative.

SIZZLERS BARBECUED PORK SHOULDER

1 pork shoulder

DRY POWDER MIX:

2 t. paprika
1 T. onion salt
1 T. garlic salt
1 T. ground basil
1 1/2 T. lemon pepper
1 T. red pepper

1 1/2 T. black pepper

BASTING SAUCE (optional):

1/2 gal. vinegar
1 qt. Super Swine Sizzlers Barbecue
    Sauce (p. 83)
8 oz. Super Swine Sizzlers Dry
    Powder Mix (recipe above)

Preheat cooker to 250 degrees. Trim all excess fat from shoulder; mix dry powder ingredients and rub into meat. Prepare a batch of basting sauce if desired.

Put meat on grill. Place a small stick of green hickory wood beside briquettes for more smoke, as desired. Keep heat between 250 degrees and 300 degrees for first 6 to 8 hours. Reduce heat and maintain at 200 to 300 degrees for remainder of time. If basting, do so about every 3 hours. Cook 14 to 16 hours total time. Shoulder is done when internal temperature reaches 170 degrees.

Serves several

COUNTRY BOY PORK TENDERLOIN

3 large pork tenderloins

MARINADE:

1 1/2 C. apple butter
1 C. white vinegar
2 1/2 T. Worcestershire sauce
2 T. brandy

1 T. soy sauce
1 T. sugar
1 t. dry mustard
1 t. salt
1/2 t. pepper
1/2 t. paprika
1 dash Tabasco sauce

Combine marinade ingredients, blend well, and pour over tenderloins. Marinate at least 2 hours, preferably overnight.

Barbecue loins for about 3 hours over semi-direct charcoal fire, turning and basting with marinade approximately every 30 minutes until done.

Serves 6-8.

BOSS HAWG

The Boss Hawg team is somewhat of a rarity in the world of barbecue competition, as all of its members (except one) are female. Team members are Linda Thomason, Randy Smith, Virginia Smith, Judy Braswell, and Linda's mother, Mabel Thomason. Chief cook Linda Thomason says her only complaint about Randy is that they can't get him to shave his legs.

The team has been competing in contests since 1981. Their first outing was the Missouri State Championship, in Kennett, Missouri, where they won First Place in Whole Hog, First Place in Shoulder, and Grand Champion. They have entered that contest every year since its inception, and have also competed in contests in Chicago, St. Louis, Memphis, Dewitt, Blytheville, and Caruthersville. Boss Hawg first entered Memphis in May in 1987 and placed Third in Ribs.

Linda states, "At first, the male teams were stunned at an 'all female' cooking team on the barbecue circuit. We have turned around that perception a bit. Barbecuers are not a sexist bunch, and kind of look out for us."

Boss Hawg is sponsored by Bull's Eye Bar-B-Que Sauce.

HAWG'S PORK LOIN BAR-B-QUE

3 pork loins
salt and pepper to taste
3/4 C. Bull's Eye Bar-B-Que Sauce

Place pork loin (fat side down) on a moderate fire and allow to cook until fat sets. Lightly sprinkle salt and pepper and wrap in foil. Set on indirect heat for approximately 45 minutes to 1 hour. Unwrap, drain off pork juices, and mix juice with barbecue sauce. Make a slit lengthwise in meat, two-thirds deep. Pour mixture into this slit and brush on sides of the meat. Re-wrap and place pork loin back on indirect heat; baste occasionally, cooking until tender.

Serves 6-8

RED GILL'S HAM

20-24 lb. fresh ham
1 (16 oz.) can sliced pineapple
1 (16 oz.) can crushed pineapple
1 (16 oz.) can applesauce
1 (8 oz.) jar maraschino cherries
1 clove garlic, peeled
1 mixture of meat sugar cure

Wash ham in cold water and trim off excess fat. Rub all over with sugar cure. Allow to set for 8 to 10 hours or overnight. Pierce to the bone with a sharp, thin knife, and push garlic clove down into crevice as close to the bone as possible. Make five to six "X" cuts across ham. Wrap in foil and place on medium hot grill for 3 hours. Do not unwrap, but turn ham over and cook for 2 more hours.

Mix crushed pineapple, applesauce, and juice from cherries. Unwrap ham and baste all over with this mixture. Rewrap and place on grill for 2 more hours. Unwrap ham and cook over grill until firm and dry outside, about 1 hour. Turn once. Using toothpicks, garnish ham with sliced pineapple and cherries.

Serve on a bed of lettuce leaves, surrounded with sliced tomatoes and onions.

Serves lots

HEAVENLY HOGS

The Heavenly Hogs are based in Jackson, Tennessee. The team consists of Jim Avent, Jimmy Ozment, John Roberts, Jack Hall, and Neil Dorris. The Hogs have been cooking in competition for eleven years and have competed at Memphis in May every year since 1978.

Chief cook Jim Avent is an avid wine and food connoisseur. He is a fifteen-year member of the International Food and Wine Society and several other wine tasting groups. Jim has traveled extensively in search of gourmet food and wines, but only has to go to his backyard for great barbecue.

The Heavenly Hogs team has won over thirty awards in barbecue contests, including Grand Champion at the Jackson, Tennessee, contest in 1986 and 1987 and at the Dyersburg, Tennessee, Homecoming Contest in 1988. The team has competed in Ireland, Nashville, Charleston, and Chicago, where they placed eleventh out of 600. The Heavenly Hogs is not a commercially sponsored team.

RED'S BARBEQUED TACOS

1 1/2 lbs. chopped barbecued pork butt or shoulder
Razorback Barbeque Sauce (mild or hot, to taste)
1/2 head lettuce, chopped
2 tomatoes, chopped
1 onion, chopped
12 taco shells

Chop meat fine and mix well with a generous amount of barbecue sauce. Fill taco shells with heated meat and top with remaining ingredients.

Serves 4-6

HEAVENLY LOIN BACK RIBS

2 slabs baby back ribs
warmed honey

DRY RUB MIX:

3 T. paprika
1 T. onion powder
1 T. garlic powder
1 T. ground basil
1 1/2 T. dry mustard powder
1 T. red pepper
1/2 T. black pepper

Combine dry rub ingredients and rub onto ribs. Cook ribs over hickory coals at 190-200 degrees for 4 to 5 hours. 15 minutes before serving, coat the ribs with heated honey.

Serves 4-6

SENATOR JIM'S CAPITOL COOKS

"Barbecue is as much a part of the Tennessee tradition as country ham, sawmill gravy, cathead biscuits, and country music. Since my earliest days, I've had a keen appetite for good barbecue and there's no better place to sample the smokey delicacy than the annual Memphis in May barbecue cook-off. Hundreds of master barbecuers gather to show off their latest sauces and to check out the competition. I might add that my own recipe, perfected over several years, usually finds favor with the tasters who stop by our tent at the cook-off." *Senator Jim Sasser*

SASSER'S BARBECUE RIBS

3-4 lbs. ribs
1 T. salt
2 onions chopped
2 T. vinegar
2 T. Worcestershire sauce
1/2 t. red pepper

3/4 C. ketchup
3/4 C. water
1 t. paprika
1/2 t. black pepper
1 t. chili powder

Sprinkle ribs with salt, then brown them on the grill. Combine remaining ingredients and use to baste the ribs. Cook at 180 degrees until tender, about 4 to 5 hours.

Serves 4-6

"RIBS THAT MAKE YOUR BREATH COME HARD"

2 slabs "third and down" ribs
Accent
garlic powder
garlic salt
onion powder
black pepper
prepared mustard
barbecue sauce

Season ribs liberally with (in this order) Accent, garlic powder, garlic salt, onion powder, and black pepper. Completely cover both sides of ribs with mustard.

Cook over medium-to-hot direct heat, 12 to 14 inches from coals, bone side down for about 2 hours. (Cook over charcoal only, no wood.) During the last 5 to 10 minutes of cooking time, glaze ribs with your favorite barbecue sauce.

For a delicious smoke flavor, toward end of the cooking process drizzle a small amount of vegetable oil around the edge of coals. Close lid and dampers completely. This produces a great deal of smoke that enhances the flavor of the ribs.

Serves 4-6

PIG DIAMONDS

Pig Diamonds is a Memphis team composed of Sam Simmons, Nancy Simmons, Marye Main, Sonja Thorsen, Karen Brehm, Greg Gang, Christine Gang, Bert Wade, Jim Moffatt, Nancy Jane Skaggs, and Annette Andreini. They have competed in Memphis in May for the past ten years in the Shoulder division.

Everyone on this team has his or her own specialty. Chief cook Sam Simmons learned to barbecue as he was growing up in Grenada, Mississippi. He is assisted in the eighteen-hour shoulder cooking process by Greg Gang and Bert Wade. Jim Moffatt's specialty is cooking breakfast on Friday morning. Nancy Simmons makes the sauces and rubs. Greg Gang designed and built the cooker from an old air compressor tank. Sonja Thorsen is in charge of slaw and Marye Main heads the baked bean, potato, and pecan cookie departments. Members not specifically mentioned do whatever else needs doing.

BIG ED'S PORK STEAKS

6 pork steaks
dry spice mix
K.C. Masterpiece Barbecue Sauce (or sauce of your choice)
1 T. garlic salt
Rendezvous spice

DRY SPICE MIX:

1 part garlic powder
1 part McCormick barbecue spice
1/2 part celery salt
1/8 part hickory-flavored salt

Rub dry spice into meat and refrigerate overnight. Grill steaks over charcoal for 30 to 45 minutes at 250 degrees. Baste with barbecue sauce, and sprinkle lightly with garlic salt and Rendezvous spice. Use a basting brush to work garlic salt and Rendezvous spice into sauce. Cook 30 more minutes and serve.

Serves 6

SMOKED PORK CHOPS

6 pork chops (1 1/2 to 2-in. thick)
salt and pepper to taste
dry barbecue seasoning mix (optional)
Kraft Thick 'n Spicy Barbeque Sauce

Heat grill to about 225 degrees. Season chops with salt and pepper or with dry barbecue mix (commercial or make your own).

Place chops in center portion of grill, maintaining a slow temperature of 225 to 250 degrees. Cook for 2 hours, turning once. Use barbecue sauce to finish meat the last 15 to 20 minutes or serve on the side.

Serves 6

HOGAHOLICS AWARD-WINNING RIBS

2 slabs ribs

DRY RUB MIX:

1 T. lemon peel
1 T. garlic powder
1 T. onion powder
1 T. chili powder
1 T. paprika
1 T. MSG (optional)
1/2 black pepper
1/2 T. cayenne pepper
1/2 T. white pepper
2 T. salt
2 T. sugar

BASTING SAUCE MIX:

4 C. Wicker's Barbecue Marinade and Baste
2 C. vegetable oil
2 C. apple cider vinegar
1/2 C. lemon juice

Skin ribs and set aside for 1 hour to reach room temperature. Combine dry rub ingredients and rub into both sides of ribs.

Place meat on grill away from coals, bone side down. Combine basting sauce ingredients. Cook ribs 1 1/2 to 2 hours before turning and using basting sauce. Cook slowly for 3 1/2 to 4 1/2 hours, basting every 45 minutes to 1 hour. Serve with barbecue sauce on the side, or (not recommended by purists) baste with barbecue sauce the last 1/2 hour.

"This recipe is guarded by killer basset hounds in a Civil War bomb shelter."

Serves 4-6

BEEF

GRILLED T-BONE STEAK

4 T-bone steaks (1 1/2-in. thick)

MARINADE:

1 C. red wine
1/2 C. Italian dressing
2 T. W'ham seasoning
cracked pepper

   Combine marinade ingredients and pour over meat; let stand for 2 hours.
   Add damp hickory chips to medium-hot coals. Cook steak for 10 to 15 minutes, basting with marinade. Turn and cook for 15 to 20 more minutes with grill cover closed. Serve with heated marinade.

   Serves 4

BARBEQUED BEEF TENDERLOIN

3-4 lb. beef tenderloin

MARINADE:

1/2 C. red wine
1/2 C. soy sauce
2 T. sesame oil
2 T. honey
2 cloves garlic, minced
1 T. ground ginger

   Trim fat from tenderloin and bring to room temperature. Combine marinade ingredients and place with tenderloin in a sealable plastic bag. Refrigerate overnight.
   Remove from marinade and cook over low fire with grill covered. Cook for 1 to 1 1/2 hours, basting and turning every 15 minutes.

   Serves 6-8

OLD MILWAUKEE'S
PADDLEWHEEL PORKERS

The Paddlewheel Porkers team was formed in 1981 in time to compete in the Fourth Annual Memphis in May Barbecue Contest. The team is sponsored by the Old Milwaukee division of Stroh Brewing Company. They are easy to locate at any contest, as their cooking space is occupied by a forty-three-foot replica of a Mississippi River paddlewheeler. The "Boat," as they affectionately refer to it, is complete with cooker, galley, two decks, and a revolving paddlewheel.

Chief cook Tom Sampson and co-ordinator Bill Thompson spent their first few barbecue competition years capturing the "Fun Award." Having declared themselves uncontested winners in the Fun category and having honed their cooking skills in the process, they decided to compete for the barbecue awards. In 1988, the Paddlewheel Porkers competed in fifteen contests and collected a total of thirty trophies, including Grand Champion at Covington, Tennessee; Caruthersville, Missouri; Tuscaloosa, Alabama; and West Memphis, Arkansas. They also were runner-up for Memphis in May Team of the Year.

The Porkers team members are Tom Sampson, Bill Thompson, John Thompson, Mike King, Rick Handwerker, and Ron Haney. One of them recently declared, "We learned something very important in 1988. Even considering the extra work required, success in cooking always brings along with it The Fun Award."

BILL THOMPSON'S SIRLOIN STEAK

2 (3-lb.) sirloin steaks (1 1/4 to 2-in. thick)

MARINADE:

1/3 C. Worcestershire sauce
1 1/2 t. garlic powder
1 1/2 t. lemon pepper

Coat steak with Worcestershire sauce and rub in dry marinade seasonings with fingers. Refrigerate marinated meat for 2 hours prior to cooking.

Sear for 2 minutes on each side on hot grill. Reduce heat to medium to low, cook to taste (rare, 4 minutes each side; medium, 6 minutes each side; well, 8 minutes or longer each side).

Serves 6-8

BBQ BEEF HOT DOGS

1 pkg. all-beef hot dogs
1 large onion, sliced
1-1 1/2 C. hickory smoke barbecue sauce

Place 4-5 hot dogs on a large piece of heavy-duty aluminum foil. Top with several slices of onion. Repeat layers and cover with barbecue sauce. Tightly close aluminum foil and place in a disposable aluminum pan. Cook over a medium-hot fire for 30 to 40 minutes. Serve on hot dog buns.

Serves 8-10

THE ARKANSAS TRAV'LERS

The Arkansas Trav'lers hail from Birdeye, Arkansas. Their chief cook and founder is Jim Quessenberry, Ph.B. (Philosopher of Barbecue), who's a farmer in his spare time. Other team regulars are Chris Burrow, Tom B. Smith, John Collier, Donna Quessenberry, Mark Smith, and Bob Stacy.

Victims of barbecue wanderlust, the Trav'lers have traveled to Cleveland, San Antonio, Daytona Beach, and even Ireland to test their barbecue cooking skills. They were 1985 and 1987 Grand Champions in the Irish Cup International Barbeque Contest in Galway Bay, Ireland. They have competed in Memphis in May every year since its inception and have placed twice. The Trav'lers have won many Memphis in May sanctioned contests over the years, including the Wynne, Arkansas Funfest, and were Grand Champions of the John Morrell "Jet Net" ham contest in 1985. In February 1989, Quessenberry and Ray "Red" Gill's Razorback Cookers joined forces to compete in the Great Southern BBQ Championship in Daytona Beach, Florida. They won Second in Shoulder, Second in Inside Round, and Third in Brisket, plus Second Place Overall. Not a bad way to start the year.

In October 1988, Quessenberry's Dry Rub rated in the "Top Three" and his "Sauce Beautiful" won a packaging award at the National Barbecue Sauce Tasting Contest in Kansas City, Missouri.

TRAV'LERS BODACIOUS BEEF BRISKET

1 10 to 12-lb. beef brisket

DRY RUB:

6 T. chili powder
4 T. salt
2 T. black pepper

Rub brisket with dry rub seasoning and cook over direct heat in covered grill at 225 degrees for 6 hours. Wrap brisket in foil and continue cooking another 4 hours. Chill, slice on a meat slicer, and then warm back up to serve.

Serves 16-18

J-R'S SPICY SMOKED ROAST BEEF

1 well-marbled chuck roast, room temperature
salt and pepper to taste
1/2 C. J-R's Basting Sauce (*p. 77*)
1/2 C. Kraft Thick 'n Spicy Barbeque Sauce with Honey
1/2 to 3/4 C. broth (reserved from roast)

Sprinkle salt and pepper on the roast and wrap tightly in heavy-duty foil. Place toward hotter end of smoker and cook about 4 1/2 hours, maintaining a temperature of about 225 to 250 degrees. Uncover and check for tenderness.

Pour accumulated broth off roast and mix with basting sauce and barbecue sauce. Make a pan under the roast from the foil and pour over the meat. Leave uncovered, making sure that water level in the smoker is sufficient to keep the meat from drying out, and close the top damper almost completely. Keep meat moist and let the flavor soak in.

Serves 6-8

CAJUN COUNTRY COOKERS

Raised in southern Louisiana, Cajun Country Cooker Darrell Hicks began cooking when he was in high school. His father passed along to him a delicious recipe for Cajun spices that made pork loin and ribs "a treat for a king." The spice worked so well in competition that Darrell started packaging it for retail sale as "Cajun Country Seasoning." Recently, he added "Cajun Country Rice" to the product line. The Cookers also have a thriving catering business.

Darrell, along with his partner Bob Knodell and their team of cookers, has won many first prize honors with his special brand of barbecue. Among the team's awards are the 1986 Grand Champion at Memphis in May, Show-Me State Champion in Kennett, Missouri, and Champion at the Annual Riverfront Picnic and International Barbecue in St. Louis.

Darrell's wife, Ann, says he loves to cook, no matter what the weather or the circumstances. He recently set a record in *The Guinness Book* for cooking 3,117 slabs of pork ribs in forty-eight hours—enough to serve 9,000 customers! Profits from the sale of those ribs went to benefit Boy's Town of Missouri, Inc.

The Cajun Country Cookers team members are Bob Knodell, Darrell Hicks, Darron Hicks, Bill Chrysler, Bill Bateman, C. C. Smith, and Alan Hedrick.

PEPPERED PORTERHOUSE STEAKS

4 porterhouse steaks
4 T. olive oil

SPICE RUB:

1 T. garlic powder
1 T. paprika
2 t. thyme
2 t. oregano
1/2 T. black pepper
1 t. lemon pepper
1 t. cayenne pepper
1 t. salt

Combine spice rub ingredients. Lightly coat steaks with oil, then rub in spice rub until well coated. Let stand at room temperature for 1 hour, then grill over hot coals for 4 to 6 minutes each side.

Serves 4

CAJUN BEEF SAUSAGE

1/2 lb. ground beef
1 T. Cajun Country Seasoning

Mix ground beef with Cajun Country Seasoning. Blend well and make into small patties. Grill over medium heat until brown. Great breakfast sausage!

Serves 4

THE POT BELLIED PORKERS

The latest members of the Memphis in May royalty are the Pot Bellied Porkers, the 1989 Team of the Year. After only two years of cooking in competition, this team is the fourth to earn the title by outscoring all other teams on the Memphis in May circuit. The Porkers are sponsored by the Campbell Soup Company of Camden, New Jersey. Team members are Alex Camacho, Mel Drewery, Janice Drewery, Frank Morgan, Willie Alcantara, Monroe James, Linda Lane, and Mary Alcantara. Five of them moved to Memphis from New Orleans in 1986, and three still comute to compete in barbecue competitions.

During their brief and stellar career, the Pot Bellied Porkers have won Grand Championships at DeWitt, Arkansas; Clarksdale, Mississippi; Southeast Memphis; McKenzie, Tennessee; and Middleburg, Florida. They have earned thirteen First Place, eleven Second Place, and eight Third Place trophies, as well as numerous other awards for showmanship and sauce competitions.

The Porkers have no plans to rest on their laurels. Alex Camacho, chief cook, intends to take their show on the road this year and expand the team's cooking horizons to the East Coast and to the Midwest. Barbecuers, beware. You never know where the Pot Bellied Porkers will turn up next!

QUESSENBERRY'S PRIME RIB

15-16 lb. standing rib roast,
  nicely marbled
1 t. garlic powder

1/4 C. olive oil
freshly cracked black peppercorns
horseradish sauce (optional)

With a boning knife, carefully separate the rib bone from the roast, keeping in one piece. Remove the "lip" or fat layer in one piece. Sprinkle the ribeye with garlic powder, then reassemble the pieces. Tie with butcher's string, binding at each rib. Brush generously on all sides with olive oil and cover entire surface with cracked pepper.

Cook on a closed grill over medium (250-degree) indirect heat. Cook for 2 to 3 hours, until internal temperature reaches 140 degrees (medium rare). Wrap roast tightly in foil to allow a little extra steaming time. Remove foil, carve into 1/2-inch thick slices; the outside will be well done and the center rare. May be served with horseradish sauce.

Serves a bundle

CAMACHO'S SPICY K-BOBS

2 lbs. chuck roast, partly frozen

MARINADE:

1 C. water
12 oz. Spicy V-8 juice
1/4 C. red wine vinegar
1 T. tomato paste

1 t. garlic salt
1/2 t. salt
1 t. black pepper
1 bay leaf
1/2 C. chopped jalapeno peppers
1 C. chopped onion

Cut meat into 1-inch squares while still partly frozen. Combine marinade ingredients and stir. Add meat and cover. Marinate for 24 hours, stirring occasionally.

Prepare shish kebabs, using 5 to 6 cubes of meat per skewer. Grill over hot coals and baste. Simmer remaining marinade for 15 minutes and serve along side cooked meat.

Serves 4

BEEF

"SHUG" POWELL'S
BARBECUED BEEF ROAST

4-4 1/2 lb. shoulder roast
2 T. shortening
barbecue sauce

MARINADE:

1/4 C. Worcestershire sauce
1/4 C. Liquid Smoke
1/4 C. lemon juice
1/4 C. soy sauce
1/2 C. vinegar
1/2 C. RC Cola
1/4 C. sugar
vegetable oil (optional)

Combine marinade ingredients in a small saucepan and cook slowly for 4 to 5 minutes, stirring to blend.

Trim fats or membranes from meat surfaces that will face coals; place with marinade in a gallon-size sealable plastic bag. Marinate meat a minimum of 2 hours on each surface. Remove from bag, pat dry, and rub 1 tablespoon shortening on each side. Pour marinade into a container and use as a basting sauce, adding additional cola to mixture if needed.

Place charcoal on one side of grill, just enough to cover a space slightly larger than meat surface. If using wood chips, put them into a container and cover with water. When coals are ash gray, place meat on grill about 2 to 3 inches over coals; sizzle for 2 minutes. Turn over and sizzle for another 2 minutes. Move roast on grill 4 to 6 inches away from edge of coals. Raise grill 6 to 8 inches, place wood chips on coals, and lower grill cover. Turn roast and baste every 15 to 20 minutes, adding wood chips and/or charcoal as needed. Roast will be done in 2 to 3 hours. Use barbecue sauce for basting both surfaces of roast during last 30 minutes of cooking.

Serves 8-10

LAMB

SPICY LAMB KABOBS

2 lbs. boneless lamb
onion wedges
green pepper squares
sweet red pepper squares

MARINADE:

1/4 C. Wicker's Marinade and Baste
1/4 C. vegetable oil
1/4 C. lemon juice
2 cloves garlic, minced
1/4 C. chopped parsley

Cut lamb into 1-inch cubes. Combine marinade ingredients and add lamb. Cover and refrigerate 6 to 8 hours. Drain meat and save marinade. Thread lamb cubes with onion and peppers on skewers. Grill over hot coals for 10 to 12 minutes and baste often with remaining marinade.

Serves 6

JOELLYN "LAMB CHOP" FORRESTER

Joellyn is a team of one, specializing in lamb. She has competed in the Irish Cup World International Barbecue Contest since its inception in 1985. Her alias in that competition is "Patty's Piglet," and she has won the Lamb division several times. She was Grand Champion of the St. Patrick's Day Stew and Que in 1987.

Joellyn is also the Tolerance Trophy winner for putting up with Silky Sullivan all these years.

JOELLYN'S AWARD-WINNING LAMB

1 leg of lamb, bone in
6-8 garlic cloves
1 (3.7 oz.) jar lemon pepper
olive oil

Prepare covered charcoal grill for cooking. Peel garlic cloves and cut into 2 to 3 slivers each. Tuck slivers into meat's natural crevices, and pierce the leg to tuck away more. Rub meat with olive oil and coat generously with lemon pepper.

Cook over medium-low coals for 3 (rare) to 4 (well done) hours. (Cooking time can be decreased by deboning lamb.) Turn over once or twice during cooking. Cook to internal temperature of 130-160 degrees.

Serves 12-15

MARINATED LAMB CHOPS

8 lamb chops

MARINADE:

1 t. paprika
1 t. dry mustard
1 t. rosemary
1 t. tarragon
2 cloves garlic, minced
1/4 C. dry white wine
2 T. honey
2 T. oil
salt and pepper to taste

Combine marinade ingredients and pour over lamb chops. Cover and refrigerate at least 2 hours. Grill and baste chops over medium-hot coals for 5 minutes each side.

Serves 4

POULTRY

TRAV'LERS CHICKEN OREGANO

3 (2 1/2 to 3 lb.) chickens, quartered

MARINADE:

1 C. lemon juice
4 C. olive oil
2 t. salt
1 t. garlic powder
1 T. dried oregano

Place chicken in a glass dish. Combine marinade ingredients and pour over meat. Cover and refrigerate for several hours.

Remove from marinade; cook over 200 to 225 degree coals in a covered grill for approximately 2 hours. Turn and baste with reserved marinade every 20 to 30 minutes until done.

Serves 10-12

ARKANSAS GOLDEN BARBEQUED CHICKEN

4 chicken fryers, cut in half and wings discarded

BASTING SAUCE:

4 C. cider vinegar
2 sticks margarine
4 t. salt
2 t. black pepper
1 t. red pepper

Mix basting sauce ingredients in a saucepan; simmer.

Place pieces of chicken on an open-pit barbeque grill and cook for approximately 1 hour, 45 minutes, turning and mopping every 15 minutes with baste. (Keep a water bottle handy; fire tends to flare up under chicken.)

Serves 8

J-R'S COOK'N'CREW

Jerry Roach designed his first barbecue pit smoker in 1979, then spent four years improving on the original design until he knew he had built the "best barbecue smoker to ever to be manufactured." In 1983, he went into full production, building smokers for individuals, fellow barbecue contestants, restaurants, and catering services. Jerry's customers will attest to the value of the J-R cooker.

Jerry began entering barbecue contests in 1983 and has won over 100 trophies and awards since then. In 1986, his was the first team ever awarded the prestigious Memphis in May Team of the Year. Other awards include 1984 Arkansas State Champion; 1985 Mississippi and Arkansas State Champion; 1986 Mississippi State Champion and Grand Champion at the St. Louis All American Barbeque Contest, Chief Black Dog International Barbecue Contest, and McKenzie Funfest; 1987 Grand Champion of Stuttgart, Arkansas, Farmfest Barbecue Contest, Southeast Memphis Barbeque Contest, and Mid-South Barbeque Contest, State Champion in Arkansas and Louisiana, and Best Pork Barbecue and Best Pork Ribs at the Pensacola World Invitational Barbeque Round-Up; and 1988 Arkansas and Louisiana State Champion.

J-R's Cook'n'Crew Team consists of Jerry, his wife Carolyn, Butch Campbell of Paragould, Arkansas, and Susan Turner of West Helena, Arkansas. They are sponsored by Kraft Barbeque Sauce and use it as a base in seven of their eleven sauces.

W'HAM WINGS

3 lbs. chicken wings (drummie & second bone)
W'ham Seasoning (Mild or Cajun Hot)
W'ham Barbecue Sauce
bleu cheese dressing

Heat grill to medium-hot (400 to 450 degrees). Put chicken and W'ham in a plastic bag; shake to coat chicken pieces. Allow to marinate at least 20 minutes.

Place meat on grill and cook directly over hot coals 4 to 5 minutes each side or until done. Serve as an appetizer with barbecue sauce or bleu cheese dressing.

Serves 15-18

J-R's SMOKED CHICKEN

3 chicken fryers, quartered or halved
salt and pepper to taste
Kraft Thick 'n Spicy Barbeque Sauce

Preheat smoker to approximately 250 degrees. Sprinkle salt and pepper on fryer pieces and place on cooker, bone side down. Maintain temperature level and cook 1 1/2 hours. Start basting chicken with barbecue sauce during the last 30 minutes. Leg bone will twist easily when the chicken is done.

Serves 6-8

PEPTO PORKERS

The Pepto Porkers cooker would appear to be a contradiction unto itself—it's a bottle of Pepto Bismol. The 3 x 9-foot cooking unit was designed to scale by chief cook Jim Blair. And, yes, it is pink and bears the familiar yellow label. It may come as no surprise that the team is sponsored by Proctor and Gamble and that their motto is "Think pink."

The Pepto Porkers have been competing since 1985. Team members are Jim and Sherril Blair, Jim and Daphne Rakowski, Jerry Moore, Debbie Gardner, Will and Gail Baugh, Maggie Conway, and Wayne Stover. Presentation is important to this group; at judging time they wear pink shirts, yellow pants, black ties, pink aprons, and fresh pink boutonnieres. They also serve the judges at a table adorned with a pink linen tablecloth, yellow linen placemats, and fine china and silver. Service includes homemade plum wine, "Chateau Blair" 1981, and concludes with cherry or strawberry ice cream in keeping with the "pink" theme.

The combination of cooking, presentation, and pink is a successful one for the Pepto Porkers. Competing since 1985, they have won Grand Championships at Forrest City, Arkansas, Southeast Memphis (three times), and West Memphis. They have won eleven First Places, eight Second Places, two Third Places, and six Showmanship awards. They have competed in Memphis in May for five years and placed in the top ten in their category every year.

Jim Blair asserts, "We have to have confidence in our cooking if we can cook out of a stomach remedy bottle." They do, and they do cook well.

TANGY PEANUT CHICKEN

2 chickens, split in half

BASTING SAUCE:

1/2 small onion, chopped fine
1 clove garlic, minced

1/4 C. olive oil
2 T. peanut butter
4 T. lemon juice
salt and pepper to taste

To prepare basting sauce, sauté onion and garlic briefly in olive oil. Add peanut butter, lemon juice, and seasoning, stirring to blend over low heat.

Grill chicken over medium hot coals for 20 to 25 minutes, bone side down; turn and cook an additional 15 to 20 minutes, basting with sauce several times during grilling. Serve heated sauce with the chicken.

Serves 4

QUAIL A LA PEPTO

4 quail or 2 Cornish hens
4 T. cornstarch
4 T. sugar
1/2 t. salt
1 t. dry mustard
1/2 t. ground ginger

1 (1 lb.) can pitted sour red cherries
1/2 C. dry sherry
1 1/2 T. slivered orange peel
1/2 C. orange juice
1/4 C. red currant jelly

Grill quail or hens 1 hour (or until done) over medium hot coals or bake in an oven at 425 degrees for 1 hour.

In a saucepan, combine cornstarch, sugar, salt, mustard, and ginger. Drain cherries and reserve the juice. Pour sherry over cherries and set aside. Add cherry juice to cornstarch mixture. Stir in orange peel, orange juice, and currant jelly. Cook over medium heat until mixture thickens. Add sherried cherries to mixture. Just before serving, pour over hens or quail.

Serve with gourmet rice and broccoli or asparagus.

Serves 2

RAZORBACK COOKERS

Razorback Cookers chief cook Ray "Red" Gill is a personality not to be forgotten, even in a sport chock full of memorable personalities. His career pursuits include rodeo cowboy, bull rider, steer wrestler, calf roper, race car driver, and agricultural pilot. From time to time, Red also is known to be a standup comic. Ever in search of a new challenge, he started barbecuing in 1976. In 1983, he began manufacturing his Razorback brand of dry, liquid, and basting barbecue sauces in Blytheville, Arkansas. Red is assisted in barbecue cooking contests and in his manufacturing business by his son, Ray Alan.

The Razorback Cookers competed in 10 contests in 1988 and placed in all of them. Highlights include winning "World's Best Baby Back Ribs" in Richmond, Virginia, Second Place in Ribs in Mansfield, Ohio, and People's Choice Award in Pensacola, Florida. The team has won five state championships, including in their native Arkansas. In 1986, they placed in three categories at the International Barbeque Cook-Off in Lisdoonvarna, Ireland. In February 1989, the Razorback Cookers were First Runner-Up to Grand Champion at Daytona Beach, Florida.

RED'S BARBEQUED TURKEY

18-24 lb. tom turkey
1 C. Ray "Red" Gill's Spice
   (or your own mixture)
3 large onions

3 Winesap apples
2 C. Ray "Red" Gill's Barbecue Sauce
2 C. red wine
1 C. pure honey

Remove giblets from thawed turkey. Rub turkey inside and out with spice mix. Make leak-proof wrap from heavy aluminum foil. Slice one onion and one apple and lay in foil wrap. Pour 1/4 cup of barbecue sauce over apples and onions. Place turkey on top of this mixture. Slice remaining onions and apples and place inside turkey. Pour 1 cup of barbecue sauce in cavity of turkey and brush outside of bird with remaining sauce. Fold foil over turkey, form a tight seal, and place on grill.

Close top of grill and cook for about 4 hours over low to moderate heat. Before removing from grill, punch a small hole in the top of the foil to let out steam. Place pan under turkey and punch hole in the bottom of the foil to allow juices to run out. Remove turkey from foil and brush well with wine and honey mixture. Place turkey directly on grill and cook over low heat for another 2 hours, basting often with wine and honey mixture.

Serve on bed of long-grain wild rice, fresh mushrooms, corn on the cob, and barbecued onions.

Serves a crowd

ORIENTAL CHICKEN WINGS

18 to 24 chicken wings

MARINADE:

1 C. soy sauce
1/4 C. sesame oil

1/2 C. sugar
3-4 cloves garlic, minced
1 T. ground ginger
salt and pepper to taste

Combine marinade ingredients and place with chicken in a sealable plastic bag for 3 to 4 hours.

Remove wings from marinade and cook over medium-low coals for 45 to 50 minutes, turning and basting with often with reserved marinade.

Serves 6-10

CHUCK
"THE MUSTARD MONSTER"
SLATEN

Chuck Slaten has disappeared from the Memphis in May circuit! Gone but not forgotten, The Mustard Monster (whose career has relocated him to Seguin, Texas) will return at strategic, unannounced times to compete against his fellow barbecuers when they least expect it.

Chuck has been competing in barbecue contests for the past eight years. He learned to cook barbecue in his native Hot Springs, Arkansas, and has refined his cooking skills in all the barbecue hotbeds—Memphis, Kansas City, and Texas. His awards include 1986 Memphis in May Grand Champion, 1984 Mid-South Fair Grand Champion, and 1983 Show-Me State Champion. In 1987 Chuck was Grand Champion at Octoberfest in Cleveland, Mississippi. He placed in Memphis in May in 1981, 1983, 1984, 1986, and 1987, and has awards too numerous to mention (but they are posted on a large sign outside his booth at contests).

Chuck and his partner, Stan Barnes, attribute their success to "superb cooking skills." They also coat their (contest) ribs with mustard after seasoning with dry spices, thus earning Chuck his "Mustard Monster" monicker. He explains, "The mustard acts as a tenderizer and browns well. My ribs are so good they make your breath come hard." When asked if he will quit barbecuing since moving to Texas, he replies, "I'll only stop when they quit raising pork."

CHUCK'S CHICKEN

1 chicken fryer, cut into pieces
1 T. Accent
1 T. salt
1 T. pepper
1 T. garlic powder
1 T. onion powder
white vinegar
barbecue sauce

Coat chicken with dry ingredients in order of listing. Place meat in a dish and cover with white vinegar (make sure all pieces are submerged). Marinate in refrigerator for 3 hours.

Remove chicken from marinade. Grill, bone side down, for 30 to 45 minutes over medium-to-hot coals. During the last 15 minutes of cooking time, glaze chicken with your favorite barbecue sauce. Chuck's Smoke Bomb (drizzle vegetable oil around the outer edge of live coals; close lid and dampers of cooker) will add additional flavor. During last 5 minutes of cooking, turn chicken skin side down and glaze again with barbecue sauce.

Serves 4

SPICY CAJUN CHICKEN

4-6 oz. boneless and skinless chicken breast
Italian dressing
Cajun Country Seasoning

Marinate chicken in Italian dressing for 24 hours. Remove from marinade and sprinkle lightly with Cajun Country Seasoning. Grill over medium fire for 15 minutes.

Makes delicious sandwiches, may be sliced and added to a salad, or can be served whole as main dish.

Serves 4

FISH AND SEAFOOD

SHRIMP QUESSENBERRY

2 lbs. shrimp, peeled and deveined

MARINADE:

2/3 C. soy sauce
1/2 C. olive oil
2 T. brown sugar
1 1/2 t. ground ginger
1 medium yellow onion minced
2 cloves garlic, minced

Combine marinade ingredients and marinate shrimp overnight in the mixture. Skewer shrimp and grill over direct charcoal heat for approximately 20 minutes.

Serves 4-6

LOW-CAL CAJUN SWORDFISH

6 swordfish fillets

MARINADE:

6 T. lemon juice
6 T. vegetable oil
2 T. Cajun Country Seasoning
2 t. lemon pepper

Combine marinade ingredients. Place swordfish in glass dish with with marinade for 2 hours, turning once.
Remove from marinade and grill over medium-hot coals for 5 to 8 minutes each side.

Serves 6

NEW ORLEANS STYLE BAR-B-QUE SHRIMP

8 lbs. large shrimp, unpeeled
1/2 lb. butter
1 C. olive oil
8 oz. chili sauce
3 T. Lea & Perrins
   Worcestershire sauce
2 lemons, sliced
4 cloves garlic, chopped

3 T. lemon juice
1 T. chopped parsley
2 T. paprika
2 T. oregano
2 T. red pepper
1 T. Tabasco sauce
3 T. Liquid Smoke
salt and pepper to taste

Wash shrimp; spread out in a shallow pan. Combine remaining ingredients in a saucepan and cook over low heat, then pour warm mixture over shrimp. Refrigerate for several hours, basting and turning shrimp every 30 minutes.

Remove shrimp from marinade and cook in pit over indirect heat at 300 degrees for 30 minutes, turning at 10-minute intervals. Serve in soup bowls, with French bread to dip in sauce.

Serves 16-20

GRILLED ORANGE ROUGHY

4 orange roughy fillets
1 stick butter, melted
juice of 1 lemon
garlic salt
Cajun seasoning (optional)

Mix butter and lemon juice. Baste fish with mixture, then sprinkle lightly with garlic salt (and Cajun seasoning, if desired). Grill over medium coals until fish flakes (about 15 minutes), basting frequently.

Serves 4

PEPTO PORKERS GRILLED SALMON

1-3 lb. salmon, with skin left on
Pam cooking oil spray

BASTING SAUCE:

1/2 lb. butter or
   margarine, melted

1 t. lemon pepper
1 t. garlic powder
2 T. lemon juice
1 T. Worcestershire sauce
2 t. parsley flakes
dash of hot sauce

Mix together basting sauce ingredients and baste both sides of salmon. Spray gas or charcoal grill with Pam. Preheat gas grill to high heat, or let coals get hot if using charcoal. Sear salmon flesh side down for 2 minutes to seal. Turn over to skin side down.

Turn gas heat down to low or spread out charcoal. Cook on low heat, skin side down, for 45 minutes or until salmon flakes with fork. Baste throughout cooking process. Remove from fire and cut into serving pieces.

Serves 6

BBQ TROUT

4 whole trout, pan dressed

DRY RUB:

2 t. barbecue seasoning
1 t. pepper
1/4 t. garlic powder

1/2 t. salt

BASTING SAUCE:

1 t. Worcestershire sauce
1/4 t. Tabasco sauce
1/2 C. melted butter or margarine

Sprinkle trout with combined dry rub ingredients. Combine basting sauce ingredients.

Place fish in well-greased wire basket and grill over hot coals for 10 minutes each side, basting often.

Serves 4

QUALITY HOGS

The Quality Hogs barbeque team hails from Memphis, Tennessee. Ed Daniels and Sonny Daniels are the chief cooks; business associates and friends make up the rest of the team.

Ed states, "We started cooking in contests in 1982. Since then we have won thirty-six trophies in barbecue contests. In 1988, we finished third in Ribs at Memphis in May, third in Whole Hog at the Mid-South Contest, and we won Grand Champion in the Mud Island Catfish Cooking Contest with barbecued catfish." We can't wait to see what 1989 has in store for the Quality Hogs.

SONNY'S BBQ SHRIMP BOIL

2 lbs. shrimp, unpeeled
1 (28 oz.) bottle Wicker's Marinade and Baste

BBQ DIP:

1 C. Wicker's Marinade and Baste
1 C. honey

In a large pan, combine entire bottle of Wicker's sauce with an equal amount of water and bring to boil. Add shrimp and let come to a second boil for 2 minutes. Remove shrimp and serve hot or cold with BBQ Dip.

Serves 4-6

BIG ED'S BARBECUED CATFISH FILLETS

2 lbs. catfish fillets (1/2-in. thick)
6 oz. Allegro marinade

DRY SPICE MIX:

3 T. garlic powder
3 T. McCormick barbecue spice
1 1/2 T. celery salt
1 t. hickory-flavored salt

Marinate fillets for 45 minutes in Allegro marinade, then rub in a light covering of dry spice mix. Place fish on charcoal-fired grill and cook over medium heat until meat becomes light and flaky.

Serves 6

"CATFISH LIL'S" BBQ CATFISHERS

Catfish Lil's BBQ Catfishers team competes only in contests that offer a Fish category. Lil Hamrick works for Pride of the Pond and promotes Mississippi pond-raised catfish.

Catfish Lil won First Place in the Fish category of the Irish Cup International Barbecue Contest, and she plans to introduce barbecued catfish to the Thai people at the 1989 Barbecue Expo in Bangkok, Thailand. Says Lil, "I've devoted my life, as long as the money's good, to promoting catfish in every form and fashion. Some call me the Amelia Earhart of catfish for promoting it all over the world. I was the first person to take it to Europe. Now I will be the first to take it to Asia. And soon I'll be taking it to all civilized nations in the world, letting them sample the taste of this Delta cuisine. After all, Pride of the Pond makes, Catfish Lil bakes, and the world waits." 'Nuf said.

CATFISH LIL'S BBQ CATFISH

6 farm-raised catfish fillets
4 T. Catfish Lil's BBQ Marinade
1 C. water

2 T. butter
1 C. sliced fresh mushrooms
6 onion rings, thinly sliced

Mix marinade and water and marinate fillets for 2 1/2 hours.

Place fish on a drip-through grill, topped with pats of butter, mushrooms, and onion slices. Cover with foil and cook at 350 degrees for 22 minutes.

Variation: Place fish and toppings in grill basket lined with foil. Poke small holes in foil and cook fillets on outdoor grill for 30 minutes, turning once.

Serves 6

ARKANSAS TRAV'LERS BARBEQUED OYSTERS

36 raw oysters
rock salt
barbecue sauce

TOPPING:

1 stick butter, melted

1/2 t. garlic powder
1/4 C. fine bread crumbs
1 t. dried oregano
2 dashes Tabasco sauce
1 t. chopped parsley
2 T. minced onions

Arrange oysters on the half shell on a bed of rock salt in a disposable shallow aluminum pan. Combine topping ingredients and place 1 teaspoon of the mixture on each oyster.

Place pan on grill and cook over indirect heat with lots of hickory smoke for approximately 30 minutes. Oysters are done when edges begin to curl. Serve as an appetizer with your favorite hot barbecue sauce.

Serves 6

J-R's PRAWNS IN LEMON BUTTER

2 lbs. large shrimp, peeled and deveined
1 C. melted butter
1/4 C. lemon juice
1 clove garlic, minced
1 t. parsley flakes
1 t. Worcestershire sauce
1 t. soy sauce
1/2 t. seasoned pepper
1/4 t. salt
1/4 t. garlic salt

Mix all ingredients except shrimp and bring to a boil. Thread shrimp onto water-soaked bamboo skewers and cook over medium-hot coals. Baste frequently with butter sauce until shrimp are opaque, 3 to 4 minutes per side.

Serves 4-6

WILD GAME

VENISON KABOBS

2 lbs. venison, cut into 1-in. cubes
1 tomato, cubed
1 onion, cubed
1 green pepper, cubed
4 skewers

MARINADE:

1/2 C. red wine
2 T. vegetable oil
2 T. honey
1 clove garlic, minced

Combine marinade ingredients, add cubed venison, and refrigerate for 2 to 3 hours.

Remove meat from marinade and thread 4 to 5 pieces on each skewer, alternating with vegetables. Grill over medium-hot coals for approximately 12 to 15 minutes, turning and basting often with marinade.

This is a very simple, colorful entree. Serve with garlic bread.

Serves 4

MAD DOG DEER HIND QUARTER

1 (12 to 15-lb.) deer hind quarter
1/2 gal. Mogan David 20-20 grape wine
2 oz. garlic powder

BBQ BASTING SAUCE:

2 C. Wicker's Marinade and Baste
1 C. honey
1 C. ketchup

Place meat in a disposable aluminum pan and add 1 quart of the wine. Cover pan with foil and refrigerate, marinating for 6 hours. Uncover, turn meat over, and sprinkle both sides with garlic powder. Add the remaining wine and recover pan with foil.

Heat grill to 250 degrees. Put pan on the grill and let meat simmer for 3 hours. Remove meat from wine sauce and lay directly on the grill. Prepare basting sauce. After cooking meat on grill for 1 hour, baste with sauce. Repeat basting every hour for 5 more hours, keeping grill at 250 degrees. Slice or chop and serve.

Serves about 30

PORK FORKERS

The Pork Forkers barbecue team gives the term "colorful" a whole new meaning. Team members are Bubba "Uncle Beaver" Norris, Harry "The Doctor" Sanders, Lee "Wad" Sanders, Margie "Wad" Kroehe, David "Kuntsler" Sanders, Richard "Lab" Brown, Gary "Japo" Brown, Bobby "Bugeye" Garner, Beverly "Bevo" Norris, and Don "Red" Berry. This cooking team consists of founders and committee members of the Possum Town Pig Fest.

This pignacious team exploded onto the barbecue circuit with Overall Grand Champion finish in 1983 at the First Annual Possum Town Pig Fest (which they organized, of course!). Having reached the pinnacle, they have gone into (semi-conscious?) cooking retirement, opting to cook only in international competitions. Two top twenty finishes in the Shoulder category at Memphis in May, along with two First Place popping tops finishes at Memphis, are among their many laurels.

The Pork Forkers invite you to visit with them at the highly successful (Memphis in May sanctioned) Possom Town Pig Fest, held each year the fourth weekend of August in Columbus, Mississippi. The Pig Fest was voted one of the top twenty tourist attractions in the Southeast in 1988. It's an event you won't soon forget!

UNCLE BEAVER'S MARINATED DUCK BREASTS

5 duck breasts, halved and deboned
Bryan's Smoky Hollow thick
    bacon slices

MARINADE:

1/2 C. soy sauce
1/2 C. red wine
1 t. garlic salt

1 t. onion salt
2 C. zesty Italian dressing
1 t. Worcestershire sauce
1/2 t. meat tenderizer
1/4 t. garlic pepper
pinch of tarragon
pinch of rosemary

Combine marinade ingredients and marinate meat a minimum of 8 hours, turning often. Remove breasts from liquid, wrap each in bacon, and brush with marinade. Char-grill as you would a small filet mignon (you may think that's what you're eating!).

Serves 8-10

RED'S BARBEQUED 'COON

1 (8 to 10-lb.) raccoon, dressed
2 medium onions, chopped
salt and pepper to taste
3 red pepper pods
Razorback Barbeque Sauce

Wash 'coon and cut up. Cover with cold water in Dutch oven. Bring to a boil for 15 minutes. Pour off this water and add fresh water, onions, salt, pepper and pepper pods. Boil 1 to 2 hours or until tender. Remove and dry on paper towels.

Dip meat in barbecue sauce and place on hot grill for 45 minutes, basting frequently. Remove from grill and place in shallow pan. Pour sauce over meat and bake at 350 degrees for 1 hour.

Serves 10-12

TEX-A-DOODLE

The Tex-A-Doodle team has been competing in barbecue competitions for nine years. The six team members (Tex Caviness, Gaines Tennison, Benny Hopper, Frank Austein, Harry Gonterman, and Bob Parker) have been friends for twenty years. They designed their own grill and then spent a year building it.

The Tex-A-Doodles have competed at Memphis in May for several years, and team assistant Sylvia Hopper has competed in the Miss Piggy contest eight times, more than any other contestant. She hasn't won yet, but keeps trying. The cooking team has placed at Memphis in May five times; they, too, intend to keep on trying. Explains social activity co-ordinator Gaines Tennison, "We go for the fun and enjoyment, and we DO try to win."

The Tex-A-Doodle team's successes include the Whole Hog division at both the Southhaven, Mississippi, and the East Memphis contests. They have no commercial sponsor. They do have a large crowd of friends on hand to cheer them on and partake of their great 'Que.

TEX'S VENISON HAM DELIGHT

whole venison ham
1 lb. bacon
barbecue sauce

MARINADE:

1 C. vinegar
5 C. water
12 T. salt
1 bottle Italian salad dressing

Clean whole ham. Combine marinade ingredients and cover approximately three-fourths of the ham with the mixture. Marinate for 12 hours, then turn meat and marinate for 12 more hours.

Drain off liquid and cover ham with bacon strips. Put in a covered pan in a 350-degree oven and bake for approximately 8 hours. Cover with fresh bacon strips periodically. To serve, chop and mix with barbecue sauce.

Serves 12-14

PORKERS VENISON TERIYAKI

1 elk or deer steak (1/2-in. thick)

MARINADE:

3/4 C. sauterne or other white wine
3 T. white vinegar
2 T. soy sauce
1/4 C. light brown sugar
1 clove garlic, minced
1/2 t. ground ginger

Combine marinade ingredients and marinate steak for at least 4 hours, turning frequently. Grill over slow heat, using marinade to baste. Cook for approximately 10 minutes per side (do not overcook).

This marinade is also good for kabobs.

Serves 2

CAJUN WILD DUCK

2 ducks (or 1 goose)
1/2 C. dry white wine
2 T. Cajun Country Seasoning

Rub bird(s) with wine. Sprinkle Cajun seasoning inside cavity and rub in all over outside of bird(s). Place in smoker away from fire and cook at approximately 350 degrees for 2 hours. Remove from grill and wrap in foil. Return to 350-degree grill and cook an additional hour or until tender.

Serves 4

CAJUN ROAST VENISON

1 (4 to 6-lb.) venison roast

MARINADE:

1/2 C. sugar
1/2 C. Worcestershire sauce
2 T. Cajun Country Seasoning

Combine marinade ingredients. Place roast in heavy-duty foil in a disposable aluminum roasting pan. Pour marinade over meat, seal foil, and refrigerate for 8 to 10 hours.

Set smoker temperature at 300 degrees. Remove roast from marinade and place in smoker. Cook for 2 1/2 to 3 hours until tender.

Serves 6-8

W'HAM WILD TENDERS

1 (4 to 6-lb.) venison tenderloin
5-6 T. W'ham Seasoning
2 C. cola or beer

AU JUS GRAVY:

2 T. flour
1 C. cold water
1 t. W'ham Seasoning
1 T. W'ham Sauce

Rub tenderloin liberally with seasoning. Refrigerate for 24 hours in a sealable plastic bag. Remove, drain, re-rub, wrap in heavy-duty foil, and place in a disposable aluminum pan. Put back in refrigerator for a minimum of 12 hours.

Remove from refrigerator. Open foil and add cola or beer to a depth of 1/2 inch. Seal foil and place in a covered grill at 225 degrees for 1 to 1 1/2 hours. Take tenderloin out of foil (save juice) and place on grill to brown for about 12 to 15 minutes on each side.

While browning meat make au jus gravy. Put reserved meat juice in a skillet. Combine flour and water in a jar and shake well. Add to juice and bring mixture to a simmer; add more water as needed to thin. Add W'ham seasoning and sauce. Serve gravy warm with sliced meat.

Serves 8-10

RUBS, MARINADES, AND SAUCES

BOSS PIT DRY BARBECUE SEASONING

13 oz. salt
2 oz. red pepper
1 1/2 oz. black pepper
1 oz. garlic powder
1 oz. chili powder
1 oz. MSG (optional)
1 T. celery salt
1 small can nutmeg or to taste
1 small can allspice or to taste
1 small can ground cloves or to taste
1 small can onion powder or to taste

Combine all ingredients and rub into meat prior to placing on the pit. This seasoning is excellent on shoulders and ribs.

POT BELLIED PORKERS RIB SEASONING

2 C. paprika
3/4 C. lemon pepper
1/4 C. white pepper
1/4 C. coarsely ground black pepper
1/4 C. onion salt
1/4 C. granulated garlic
1/4 C. chili powder
3/4 C. brown sugar

Mix all ingredients and rub into meat prior to cooking.

HOGAHOLICS

The Hogaholics began their barbecue career at the 1978 Memphis in May contest. They haven't missed a year since, and they placed Fourth in the Rib Category in 1987. The team also participates in other contests on the "circuit," and the members are most proud of their performance at the Knoxville Riverfeast, where they were Grand Champion in 1985, 1986 and 1987.

The Hogaholics are Fred Fink (chief cook), Jim Garts, Jim Marty, Jon Hobart, Gary Easter, Norm Wilcox, Gary Ball, Roger Sapp, and other associated outlaws and hoodlums.

When asked to reveal the secrets of their success, team member and social chairman Jim Marty states, "We get together and try to decide what we can agree upon. It's a contest in and of itself. Our secret ingredient is diluted battery acid, dried in the sun and stored in the basement, guarded by two killer basset hounds. It may not the the best barbecue sauce you ever ate, but it will sure start your engine on a cold morning."

In February, some of the team traveled to Bangkok, Thailand, on a field trip to introduce barbecue to the Thai. Jim relates, "In Thailand we barbecued an elephant, but didn't do well because only four members attended and we couldn't figure out how to turn it. The Thai were in awe that Americans knew how to cook spicy food." A good time was had by all.

HOGAHOLICS DRY RUB

1 T. lemon peel
1 T. garlic powder
1 T. onion powder
1 T. chili powder
1 T. paprika
1 T. MSG
1/2 T. black pepper
1/2 T. cayenne pepper
1/2 T. white pepper
2 T. salt
2 T. sugar

Combine all ingredients and rub into meat before cooking.

SUPER SWINE SIZZLERS DRY POWDER MIX

2 T. paprika
1 T. onion salt
1 T. garlic salt
1 T. ground basil
1 1/2 T. lemon pepper
1 T. red pepper
1 1/2 T. black pepper

Combine all ingredients and rub into meat before cooking.

BOSS PIT

Boss Pit is a Memphis team composed of Charles Custer, Tom Scott, Jerry Campbell, Grady Jones, and George Steffens. All of the members are local businessmen committed to the elevation of partying and "Bar-B-Queing" to an art form. Their four-day revelries during the Memphis in May festival attest to their success in the pursuit of the "ultimate good time."

Led by Tom Scott, chief cook and party facilitator, the Boss Pit team placed Third in the Shoulder division during the 1988 Memphis in May barbecue contest. In addition, they were presented a trophy declaring Boss Pit the "Mound Bayou Grand National Barbecue and Break Dancing Champions," an honor for which they swear they were totally undeserving.

Quotes team member Charles Custer, "If we can all remain free men and stay out of the clutches of those who would curtail our revelries, we will once again put on our Ultimate Party (at Memphis in May) in 1989 at the south end of Tom Lee Park. However, in case you don't get the opportunity to sample some of our 'pluperfect' barbecue, try our recipes in this book."

The Boss Pit motto: "Laissez les bon temps rouler!"

"RED" BERRY'S PORK AND CHICKEN MARINADE

10 pkgs. dry regular Italian dressing
6 pkgs. dry garlic
1/2 gal. vegetable oil
4 C. white vinegar
2 C. water
4 oz. Swain's Hickory Smoke Sauce
2 T. lemon pepper

2 T. celery salt
1 T. hickory smoke salt
6 oz. teriyaki sauce
6 oz. Tiger sauce
1 T. garlic salt
1 T. onion salt
1 (14 oz.) bottle Worcestershire sauce

Mix all ingredients well. Marinate a favorite cut of meat covered in this sauce in an insulated beer cooler for a minimum of 24 hours. Unsurpassed with shoulder, butts, or ribs.

Yields approx. 1 gallon

BOSS PIT BASTING SAUCE

1/3 C. honey
8 medium white onions, chopped fine
12 C. water
4 C. cider vinegar
8 t. Tabasco sauce
1/3 C. soy sauce
3 lbs. margarine

1/2 C. flour
8 t. salt
4 t. black pepper
1/3 C. Heinz "57" sauce
1/3 C. A-1 sauce
1/3 C. Worcestershire sauce
2 t. lemon juice

Place all ingredients in food processor and mix well. Simmer in a saucepan over low heat for 1 hour, stirring often. Use this to baste meat while cooking. All ingredients can be adjusted to taste. Experiment!

Yields 1 1/2 gallons

MATT FISHER, PRIME GREEK SWINE

Matt Fisher, Prime Greek Swine, was brought up on barbecue. He says, "Barbecue has always been in my blood. All anyone had to do was just say, 'Hey, Fish, let's BBQ', and I would grab my smoker, go get a shoulder or some ribs, and we would smoke 'em all day. You know, like some guys go fishin'."

Matt's barbecuing internship was served at Memphis State University, where he was the chief cook for his fraternity's annual pig roast. They pit smoked eight to ten shoulders overnight, and served a hundred or so revelers the next day. Those still conscious to partake of the feast rave on. The Prime Greek Swine has shared his "secret" seasoning here.

MATT FISHER'S SEASONING MIX

2 T. plus 1 t. chili powder
1 T. plus 1 t. paprika
2 t. dried oregano
1/2 t. sugar
1/2 t. dry mustard
1/2 t. ground cloves
1/2 t. celery seed
1/2 t. garlic powder
1/2 t. black pepper
1/4 t. cayenne pepper
1/4 t. thyme
1/4 t. tarragon
1/4 t. salt
1/4 t. MSG
2 bay leaves, crushed

Combine all ingredients, mix well, and put in an empty spice jar with holes in the top. Shake a fair amount onto a slab (or slabs) of ribs. Put in smoker and use a vinegar-based baste (like Wicker's). When meat is done, shake more of the seasoning on ribs and serve.

RAZORBACK COOKERS BARBEQUE SPICE

1/4 C. sugar
1/8 C. seasoning salt
3 T. pepper
3 T. paprika
3 T. chili powder
1 t. garlic powder

Combine all ingredients and rub into meat before cooking.

HOGAHOLICS BASTING SAUCE

4 C. Wicker's Marinade and Baste
2 C. vegetable oil
2 C. apple cider vinegar
1/2 C. lemon juice

Combine all ingredients. Warm and use to baste meat every 45 minutes to 1 hour during cooking.

Yields 1/2 gallon

HOLY SMOKERS, TOO BASTING SAUCE

1 gal. apple cider vinegar
1 qt. Worcestershire sauce
10 oz. lemon juice
3 heaping T. black pepper

Mix all ingredients in a large pot and bring to a hard boil for 10 minutes.

This is an old-fashioned, true Southern-style basting sauce, excellent on chicken and large cuts of pork (Boston butt, shoulders, hams, whole hog, pork roasts, etc.) The meat should be cooked over a slow fire (200 to 210 degrees) and basted every 20 to 30 minutes (not during the last hour for large pieces of meat).

Yields 1 1/2 gallons

J-R's BASTING SAUCE

1 qt. apple cider vinegar
1 t. garlic powder
1 t. poultry seasoning
6 bay leaves
1 t. crushed red pepper
1 t. thyme
1 t. rosemary
1 t. lemon pepper

Mix all ingredients and bring to a rolling boil. Cover and let mixture cool completely. Use this with any recipe that calls for a basting sauce.

Yields 1 quart

SUPER SWINE SIZZLERS BASTING SAUCE

1 qt. vinegar
1 pt. water
1/2 small can chili pepper
1/2 pt. prepared mustard
10 oz. brown sugar
1/2 stick butter
1/2 bottle root beer

Combine firts four ingredients in a saucepan and mix well. Cook very slowly for 1 hour. Add brown sugar, butter, and root beer to the mixture and slow boil for 30 minutes. Recommended for pork and wild game.

Yields 1/2 gallon

BOSS PIT SERVING SAUCE

1/2 t. red pepper
1 C. light brown sugar
1 t. dry mustard
1 small bottle Griffin's Hot-Sweet
   mustard
2 t. Liquid Smoke
2 t. teriyaki sauce
1/2 C. lemon juice
1/2 C. soy sauce
4 T. flour mixed with water
4 cloves garlic, minced
4 medium onions, chopped
1 lb. butter
4 (10 oz.) bottles Worcestershire sauce
2 T. celery, chopped
16 oz. salad oil
2 T. rosemary
2 (10 oz.) bottles A-1 Sauce
2 T. dry parsley flakes
2 (6 oz.) cans tomato paste

2 T. thyme
2 (16 oz.) bottles ketchup
2 T. basil
2 (16 oz.) bottles cider vinegar
2 T. sage
8 lemons, quartered
2 T. oregano
2 (9 oz.) jars Dijon mustard
4 bay leaves
2 T. red pepper
2 t. marjoram
2 T. black pepper
1 C. red wine
2 T. salt
20 drops Tabasco sauce
6 T. sugar
4 t. paprika
2 T. chili powder
2 jiggers bourbon

In a large pot, combine red pepper, brown sugar, mustards, Liquid Smoke, teriyaki sauce, lemon juice, soy sauce, and flour/water. Mix well and simmer until thick. Sauté garlic and onions in butter until tender, then add to previous mixture. Add remaining ingredients and enough water to make 2 gallons of sauce. Heat sauce and simmer for approximately 1 1/2 hours.

Serve sauce warm over pulled shoulder or on the side. All ingredients can be adjusted to taste. (Most sauces will taste different each time you prepare them due to the age of spices, etc.) Don't be afraid to adjust quantities or add spices to your liking.

Yields 2 gallons

POT BELLIED PORKERS BAR-B-QUE SAUCE

14 oz. Campbell's ketchup
3 T. Lea & Perrins Worcestershire sauce
1/2 C. red wine vinegar w/garlic
6 oz. Spicy V-8 juice
1 T. prepared mustard
1 t. sugar
1/8 C. light corn syrup
1 C. Kraft Original Barbeque Sauce
1/4 t. ginger
1/4 t. white pepper
1/2 t. W'ham Seasoning (hot)

Combine all ingredients in a saucepan and simmer for 1 hour.

Yields approx. 1 quart

PADDLEWHEEL PORKERS
SECOND-PLACE SAUCE

2 (40 oz.) bottles Kraft Hickory Smoke Barbeque Sauce
1 (28 oz.) bottle Wicker's Marinade and Baste
3 C. ketchup
2 T. onion juice
1 1/2 C. brown sugar
2 T. white pepper

Mix barbecue sauces. In a separate pan, combine remaining ingredients and bring to a boil. Blend with sauce mixture. Apply to both sides of barbecue product 20 minutes prior to removal from grill. Serve warm as a finishing sauce—*not* to be used for basting.

Yields approx. 1 gallon

HOLY SMOKERS, TOO

The Holy Smokers, Too have been competing in barbecue contests since 1981. Team members are Rick and Charlotte Cooper, Ernie and Mary Freeland, Rock and Sally Zanda, Patty Ramsey, Jimmie and Elizabeth Madden, Mike and Jenette Devois, John and Jeanne Louise Perry, and Chuck and Susan Osborne. Their sixteen offspring, ranging in age from eight months to twenty-one years, also assist. The Smokers attribute their success to their longstanding friendship and the desire to excel in their hobby. The Holy Smokers, Too are one of only three teams ever to win Memphis in May more than once (in 1985 and 1988), and they are the only two-time winners who are still active on the barbecue "circuit."

Since 1985, the Smokers have competed in twenty-four contests, won seven Grand Championships, thirteen First Place trophies, eight Second Place trophies, and two Third Places. They have no plans to "retire" from competition and open a barbecue restaurant.

In addition to competing in barbecue contests, the Smokers have sponsored and run the Southeast Memphis Babecue Cooking Contest since 1984 and have cooked for various church, civic, and charitable events in the Memphis area. The Smokers were featured in the opening event of Tennessee's Homecoming '86 by cooking and serving their brand of world champion barbecue for all who attended the opening ceremonies at the Pink Palace Museum.

WHISKEY-A-GO-GO SAUCE

1 t. dry mustard
2 C. ketchup
1/2 C. bourbon, or to taste
1/2 C. sorghum molasses
1/2 C. cider vinegar
2 T. Worcestershire sauce
2 T. Pickapeppa sauce

2 T. lemon juice
1 T. soy sauce
2 cloves garlic, crushed
1/2 t. coarsely ground black pepper
1 T. dried parsley
Tabasco sauce to taste

In a saucepan, make a paste of the dry mustard and a little of the ketchup. Gradually add the rest of the ketchup, stirring constantly. Stir in the rest of the ingredients. Bring to a boil over medium heat and simmer for 10 minutes. If a hotter sauce is preferred, add Tabasco to taste.

Yields 1 quart

HOLY SMOKERS, TOO SERVING SAUCE

1/2 lb. butter
3 oz. lemon juice
2 oz. soy sauce
2 oz. Louisiana hot sauce
2 t. dry mustard
1 1/2 t. garlic powder
1 t. basil
1 t. red pepper
1 t. chili powder
1 t. ginger
1/2 C. brown sugar

3 oz. white vinegar
2 oz. Worcestershire sauce
3 dashes Tabasco sauce
1 1/2 t. onion powder
1 t. allspice
1 t. black pepper
1 t. celery seed
1 t. dill weed
1 t. oregano
18 oz. tomato-base barbecue sauce
   (plain)

Melt the butter in a medium saucepan over low heat. Add the liquid ingredients next, and then stir in the other ingredients one at a time. Add the commercial barbecue sauce last. Simmer for 30 minutes, stirring often.

This sauce is best when aged at least 2 days in the refrigerator.

Yields 1 quart

SUPER SWINE SIZZLERS

The Sizzlers arrive on the barbecue scene with their own caravan. First rolls in the 28-foot trailer with galley, bunk, and storage area that still allows room in which to present their prize-winning barbecue. Next comes the trailer that contains three large cooking units plus a canopy for much needed shade. Finally appears the bus carrying the regular team members—Jim Turner, J. B. Cole, Tommy Butler, Gene Langdon, Warren Rogers, Roy Thweatt, John Traugh, Jimmy Blackford, James Lantrip, Larry Doudna, Tim Verner, and Jerry Thomas—and any alternates who want to participate.

The Super Swine Sizzlers were awarded Cooking Team of the Year for 1987 by Memphis in May at the 1988 event. In 1988, they earned Grand Championships at Southaven, Mississippi; Blytheville, Arkansas; Wynne, Arkansas (Funfest); and Parkin, Arkansas (Riverboast Festival). In 1987, the Sizzlers entered ten contests in the Shoulder division only and won nine First Places, one Second Place, and six Grand Championships. They have won First Place trophies in Memphis in May in 1985 and 1987.

Chief cook Jim Turner attributes the team's success to the right mix of Dry Powder Seasoning, slow cooking (24 hours) at even temperature (250 to 300 degrees), fresh green hickory sticks for smoke, his custom designed and built cooker, and the indirect heat cooking method. Generally, two to four team members stay up all night tending the meat and fire, and others rotate shifts and duties. It's obviously a combination that pays off.

SUPER SWINE SIZZLERS BARBECUE SAUCE

8 oz. vinegar
1 gal. barbecue sauce
4 oz. prepared mustard
8 oz. lemon juice
1 (12 oz.) can beer
8 oz. Worcestershire sauce
1 stick butter

Combine all ingredients in a saucepan. Bring to a boil and simmer mixture for 1 hour. (If a sweeter taste is desired, add brown sugar.)

Yields approx. 1 1/2 gallons

CHUCK SLATEN'S FINISHING SAUCE

1/2 C. Johnny Fair syrup (or other dark syrup)
1 C. ketchup
1/2 C. juice from container of jalapeno peppers
1 stick butter (do not substitute margarine)
3 T. dark brown sugar
1/4 C. apple cider vinegar
dash of salt

Combine and simmer ingredients in a saucepan. If mixture becomes too thick, cut with more cider vinegar. Do not boil. Top meat with this sauce during the last 5 to 10 minutes of cooking time.

Yields 1 1/2 pints

HOGAHOLICS WET SAUCE

1 (10 oz.) bottle dark soy sauce
1 (46 oz.) can tomato juice
1 (10 oz.) bottle Worcestershire sauce
1 (24 oz.) bottle ketchup
2 C. apple cider vinegar
2 C. brown sugar
2 lemons juiced
2 t. red pepper

2 t. black pepper
2 t. dry mustard
1 t. garlic powder
1 t. onion powder
1 t. oregano
1 t. allspice
1 t. ginger
1 t. basil

Mix all ingredients in a saucepan and simmer for 1 hour. Let sauce stand for 2 hours before serving.

Yields 1 gallon

SUE WARD'S TABLE SAUCE (FOR WHOLE HOG)

13 lbs. tomato sauce
7 lbs. ketchup
1 fifth Southern Comfort
1/2 C. Italian seasoning
1 C. oil
3 C. apple cider vinegar
2 C. water
6 lemons, sliced

1/4 C. garlic powder
1/2 C. onion powder
3/4 C. cayenne pepper
1/2 C. lemon peel
1/4 C. celery seed
3 (5 oz.) bottles Liquid Smoke
5 to 8 celery tops
2 lbs. brown sugar or grape jelly

Combine and simmer everything but brown sugar for about 6 hours, then add sugar. Simmer another hour or so. Remove lemon and celery tops and bottle before serving. Serves 150 for a whole hog dinner.

Yields 2 1/2 gallons

SILKY SULLIVAN'S IRISH SAUCE

1/2 gal. Paddy's Irish whiskey
1 pig

Baste pig for 2 1/2 hours in Irish whiskey. Turn over and baste again for 2 1/2 hours. Remove pig from pan, reserving whiskey. Throw away the pig and drink the sauce.

Note: Do not breathe around live coals, leprechauns, or fly any airplanes for 2 days.

BREADS

CHEDDAR CORN BREAD

1 1/2 C. yellow corn meal
1 T. baking powder
1 t. salt
3 eggs
1 C. cream-style corn
1/2 C. vegetable oil
1 C. buttermilk
2 (3 1/2 oz.) cans jalapeno peppers, chopped
1/2 large green bell pepper, seeded and chopped
1 C. shredded cheddar cheese

Mix all ingredients except cheese in a mixing bowl. Stir just until moistened. Pour half of batter into a 9-inch square greased and floured baking pan. Cover with cheese. Top with remaining batter and bake at 375 degrees for 40 minutes or until golden brown.

Serves 6-8

DEE'S SPOON BREAD

1 1/2 C. yellow cornmeal
1 1/2 C. cold milk
3 C. scalded milk
3 T. vegetable oil
1 1/2 t. baking powder
1 1/2 t. salt
6 eggs, separated

Combine cornmeal and cold milk and let sit. Add the cornmeal mixture to the scalded milk and cook in a saucepan until thick. Let cool, then add oil, baking powder, salt, and egg yolks. Pour into a soufflé dish. Beat egg whites and fold into mixture. Bake at 325 degrees for 1 hour.

Serves 6-8

GEORGE'S BREAD

1 loaf good Italian bread
1 stick butter, softened to room temperature
1/3 C. Ranch-style dressing
1/4 C. finely chopped fresh garlic
1 C. chopped green onions
1/4 C. finely chopped parsley
paprika
grated Parmesan cheese

Cut bread in half lengthwise. Mix butter with dressing, then blend garlic, onions, and parsley (combination should still be the consistency of soft butter). Spread mixture on bread and sprinkle with paprika (to color). Add Parmesan cheese to taste.

Wrap loaf in foil and place to the side on the grill. Cook for 20 to 25 minutes.

Serves 6-8

PORKERS PARMESAN TOAST

1 loaf Italian bread, cut into 1-in. slices
1/2 C. butter
1/2 C. cooking oil
1 T. garlic powder
3/4 C. grated Parmesan cheese

Melt butter in a saucepan, then add oil and garlic powder. Cook mixture until color changes slightly. Dip one side of each slice of bread in the liquid, then place on a cookie sheet. Sprinkle generously with grated cheese. Toast in oven or on the grill until golden brown. Serve hot!

Serves 6-8

"SHUG'S" BARBECUE BREAD
(From scratch!)

7 T. barbecue sauce
1 large egg
2 T. melted butter
3 C. self-rising flour
1/2 t. McCormick's barbecue spice
1 (1/4 oz.) pkg. dry yeast
4 T. sugar
1 (12 oz.) can beer at room temperature

SPREAD MIX:

2 T. barbecue sauce
1 large egg
1 T. cold water
1 T. melted butter

BASTING SAUCE:

2 T. barbecue sauce
2 T. melted butter

Preheat oven to 350 degrees. Combine barbecue sauce, egg, and butter and set aside. In a large bowl, blend flour, barbecue spice, yeast, sugar, and beer. Stir first mixture into the second; blend until smooth.

Pour dough into a greased 3 x 5 x 9-inch glass baking dish. Prepare spread mix and smooth over top of bread dough. Bake on bottom shelf of oven for exactly 35 minutes. Move dish up to second shelf from top of oven and bake for another 27 minutes.

Combine basting sauce ingredients. Remove bread from oven and baste with mixture. Cover bread in dish with foil; let cool for 2 hours. Remove foil and cool for 2 more hours before removing from container. To serve, slice off ends of loaf and discard. Cut loaf into 1 1/4 to 1 1/2 inch slices. Butter both sides thinly and toast until slightly brown.

Serves 6-8

SIDE DISHES

ARKANSAS TRAV'LERS HICKORY SMOKED PECANS

4 C. unsalted fresh pecan halves
3 T. Worcestershire sauce
3 T. peanut oil
garlic salt to taste

Combine Worcestershire sauce and oil. Pour mixture over nuts and stir until completely coated. Arrange pecans in one layer in disposable aluminum pans. Poke several holes in bottom of pans to drain off any excess oil. Roast over indirect smoky heat until done, approximately 30 minutes. Sprinkle with garlic salt and serve hot.

Serve as an appetizer

PADDLEWHEEL PORKERS SUPER SLAW

1 head cabbage, shredded or chopped
1 onion, diced
3/4 C. sugar
3/4 C. cooking oil
1 C. white vinegar
1 T. dry mustard
1 T. celery seed
1 T. salt

In a large bowl, layer (in order) cabbage, onion, and sugar. Combine remaining ingredients in a saucepan and bring to a boil. Immediately pour over layered ingredients. *Do not stir.* Allow to cool, then refrigerate overnight. Stir before serving. *For color, dice or shred several carrots and add to cabbage layer.*

Serves 6-8

SUPER SWINE SIZZLERS SLAW

1 head of cabbage
1 apple, unpeeled
mayonnaise
salt and pepper to taste
sugar (optional)

Chop cabbage and apple with peel. Moisten with mayonnaise to desired consistency. Add salt, pepper, and sugar to taste.

Serves 6-8

CUSTER'S SLAW

3/4 lb. cabbage, shredded
1/4 lb. chopped carrot
1/4 C. minced white onion
1 C. salad oil
1/2 C. sugar
1/2 C. white vinegar
1 t. dry mustard
1/2 t. red pepper
salt to taste

Combine all ingredients in a glass bowl and let marinate a minimum of 6 hours (overnight is best). Drain thoroughly and serve on barbecue sandwiches or on the side. This recipe can be doubled, tripled, etc.

Serves 4

RAINBOW PASTA SALAD

1 (12 oz.) pkg. rainbow rotini
1 C. sliced celery
1/2 C. sliced green onion
1/2 C. chopped green pepper
1/2 C. sliced green olives
   with pimentos

1/2 C. chopped pitted black olives
2 T. finely chopped parsley
1 1/2 C. mayonnaise
2 to 3 T. wine vinegar, to taste
salt and freshly ground black pepper
   to taste

Cook rotini according to package directions. Drain and place in a large bowl. Add celery, green onions, green pepper, green and black olives, and parsley and toss well. In a separate bowl, mix mayonnaise and vinegar until smooth. Add to first mixture, along with salt and pepper. Toss well. Refrigerate several hours before serving.

Serves 8

GEORGIA'S PASTA SALAD

1 lb. small shell pasta
   (such as cavatelli)
2 t. best-quality olive oil
1 1/2 t. salt
1/4 C. milk
1/2 C. sour cream
1 1/2 C. mayonnaise

2 T. beef bouillon crystals
2 green peppers, chopped
1/2 C. red onion, chopped
2 fresh tomatoes, peeled and chopped
6 sweet pickles, chopped
1 t. white wine vinegar
fresh dill, cracked pepper for garnish

Bring oil, salt, and water to a rolling boil. Add pasta, cook until tender but firm to the bite. Rinse and drain. Transfer to a bowl, add milk to moisten, toss. Set aside.

Combine sour cream and mayonnaise. Add bouillon crystals and salt to taste. Combine with pasta and toss. Add peppers, onion, tomatoes, pickles, and vinegar. Chill, covered, overnight. Toss before serving. Garnish with fresh dill and cracked pepper. (This is best prepared a day ahead.)

Serves 8

LOIS'S CORN SALAD

1 (24 oz.) pkg. frozen corn, thawed
1 C. chopped cucumber
1 C. halved cherry tomatoes
1/4 C. chopped onion
1/3 C. sour cream
2 T. mayonnaise
1 T. lemon juice
1/2 t. dry mustard
salt to taste

Combine corn, cucumber, tomatoes, and onion. Mix remaining ingredients and add to corn mixture. Chill before serving.

Serves 6 to 8

JANIE JO'S POTATO SALAD

3 lbs. new potatoes, unpeeled
1 C. sour cream
2/3 C. mayonnaise
1 T. chopped fresh dill
2 t. chopped fresh parsley
salt and pepper to taste

Boil potatoes until fork tender. Cut and slice potatoes, leaving skins on. Combine other ingredients and add potatoes while they are still warm. Refrigerate overnight.

Serves 8

MARINATED TOMATOES

6 medium tomatoes, wedged

MARINADE:

1/2 C. vegetable oil
1/4 C. white wine
1/4 C. vinegar
2 T. fresh chopped chives
2 T. fresh chopped parsley
1 clove garlic, minced
1 T. sugar
1 t. salt

Combine marinade ingredients and mix well. Add tomato wedges; cover and chill overnight.

Serves 6

J-R's SMOKER COOKED BEANS

7 (1 lb.) cans pork and beans
1 C. chopped onion
3/4 C. chopped bell pepper
2 1/2 C. ketchup
3/4 C. Worcestershire sauce
3/4 C. brown sugar
3/4 C. honey
1 lb. bacon, diced and partially cooked

Mix all ingredients well and pour into a disposable aluminum pan. Keep temperature around 275 degrees and cook beans uncovered on hot end of smoker 3 to 4 hours or until liquid is cooked down.

Serves 20-25

DONNA'S BAKED BEANS

3 (15 oz.) cans pork and beans, drained
1/2 C. chopped onions
1/2 C. brown sugar
1 C. ketchup (or barbecue sauce)
1 lb. Kielbasa, sliced (may substitute barbecue pork or smoked sausage)

Combine all ingredients and put in suitable oven-proof dish. Bake at 350 degrees until thick and bubbly (approximately 45 minutes).

Serves 10-12

TEX-A-DOODLE BBQ BEANS

2 lbs. barbecued pork shoulder
1 gal. pork and beans
2 oz. Lea & Perrins Worcestershire sauce
1 C. mixed bacon grease and chopped onions
3 oz. ketchup
1 1/2 oz. dry white wine
1 jigger bourbon
3 oz. light beer
3 oz. cola
10 oz. barbecue sauce

Combine all ingredients except pork shoulder in a large pot or kettle and mix thoroughly. Set over low heat until hot, stirring very little. Chop up barbecued shoulder, removing all fat and skin, and mix gently into steaming beans. Thoroughly heat and serve.

Serves 20

CAJUN BBQ BEANS

1 lb. mild pork sausage
2 (15 oz.) cans pork and beans
1/3 C. brown sugar
1/3 C. molasses
1/4 C. chopped bell pepper
1/2 C. chopped onion
2 T. Worcestershire sauce
1/4 C. ketchup
1 T. mustard
1 T. Cajun Country Seasoning (or more to taste)

Brown and drain pork sausage; combine with all other ingredients. Cook for 6 hours in a crockpot or bake in a 350-degree oven about 1 hour.

Serves 6

BOOTHEEL BLACKEYED PEAS

3 medium fresh jalapeno peppers, chopped
3 medium onions, chopped
1 lb. ham, diced
1/2 C. shortening
1 gal. blackeyed peas
2 smoked ham hocks

Brown jalapenos, onions, and diced ham in shortening until onions become translucent. Add blackeyed peas and ham hocks. Bring mixture to a boil and simmer for 2 hours. Great with any kind of barbecue!

Serves 6-8

J-R's SMOKED RICE

2 1/2 C. long grain rice, uncooked
6 C. chicken broth
1 (10 3/4 oz.) can Campbell's
  beef broth
1/2 C. chopped celery
1/3 C. chopped bell pepper
2/3 C. chopped onion

1 oz. Worcestershire sauce
3/4 t. thyme
1/4 t. rosemary leaves
3/4 t. garlic powder
1/4 t. pepper
salt to taste
1/2 stick butter

Combine rice, broth, vegetables, and spices in a disposable aluminum pan. Cut butter up into mixture. Cover with foil and cook on smoker at about 275 degrees until all liquid is absorbed, 1 1/2 to 2 hours (length of time will depend on how hot cooker is). Uncover, stir, move to the cooler end of the cooker and let smoke at least 1 hour, stirring occasionally.

Serves 10

HOLY SMOKERS, TOO RED BEANS AND RICE

1 lb. dry red kidney beans
2 qts. cold water
2 ham hocks
2 medium onions, chopped
1/2 green bell pepper, chopped
1 C. chopped celery
4 dashes Tabasco sauce
3/4 t. black pepper

3/4 t. cayenne pepper
3/4 t. oregano
3/4 t. thyme
1/2 t. salt
1 small bay leaf
2 small garlic pods
Minute Rice for 6, uncooked
1/2 lb. Andouille sausage, cut in pieces

Wash beans and place them in 1 quart of the cold water in a 6-quart pan. Boil for 2 minutes, remove from heat, and let stand for 1 1/2 hours.

Drain beans and return, along with next 12 ingredients, to a pan filled with remaining quart of cold water. Bring to a boil, then lower heat and simmer until ham hocks and beans are tender. Remove ham hocks and cut into small pieces. Return to pan with beans. Once again bring to a boil and add rice (plus more water if necessary) and sausage. Cook for 10 minutes. Set aside for 8 minutes. Adjust salt and pepper to taste.

Serves 8

CAJUN COUNTRY RICE

2 C. water
1 T. margarine
1/2 t. salt
1 pkg. Cajun Country Rice Mix

Bring water, margarine, and salt to a boil. Add rice mix and stir well. Turn heat down; cover and cook over low heat for 25 minutes or until water is absorbed and rice is tender. (For large amounts of rice, stir occasionally.)

Variations: Add one of the following to water when adding rice: 1 lb. pork sausage or ground beef (browned and drained), 1 lb. fresh shrimp or crabmeat (or 2 small cans), chopped cooked chicken or wild game, or 2 cups sliced smoked or Polish sausage. For additional flavor, add 1/2 teaspoon of Cajun Country Seasoning per cup of rice. For a baked casserole, simply cook rice and meat separately and mix together with 1/2 can of cream of mushroom or chicken soup; bake in a greased casserole for 20 minutes.

Serves 4-6

JIM'S POTATO-ONION FRY

5 lbs. white potatoes
5 lbs. red onion (*must* be red), sliced
cooking oil
salt to taste

Cut each potato into 8 equal wedges, leaving skins on. Deep fry potatoes in hot oil. When they just begin to brown, add onions. Cook until potatoes are crisp. Remove from oil, sprinkle lightly with salt, and serve.

Serves 10-12

BOSS HAWG'S BAR-B-QUE POTATOES

2 lbs. medium red potatoes
1 large sweet onion, halved and sliced
1-2 sticks butter or margarine
2 T. Bull's Eye Bar-B-Que Sauce
salt and pepper to taste
Velveeta cheese

Wash potatoes and cut 3 to 4 times, three-fourths of the way through. Fan out. Place a slice of onion in each cut. Melt butter and then add barbecue sauce. Place each potato on a square of foil; pour mixture over potato, add salt and pepper, and wrap foil tightly. Place on grill and let cook until done, about 30 minutes. Remove from foil and add a wedge of Velveeta, allowing cheese to melt before serving.

Serves 6-8

MARYE'S STUFFED POTATOES

8 baking potatoes
shortening
1 stick butter
salt and pepper, to taste
chives or chopped green onions (optional)

Scrub potatoes and prick with fork. Coat with shortening. Bake at 450 degrees for 45 minutes to 1 hour or until tender. Remove from oven and cut in half lengthwise. Using a kitchen towel, grasp hot potatoes and remove pulp (a melon baller or serrated grapefruit spoon works well). Beat potato pulp with butter. Add salt to taste and lots of pepper. Add chives or chopped green onions, if desired. Stuff pulp back into skins. Wrap in foil and freeze.

Place on grill over indirect heat about 3 to 4 hours before serving; turn occasionally.

Serves 8

JAMES LOWELL'S STOLEN POTATOES

2 lbs. small new potatoes
2 T. crab boil
1 T. salt
1 t. cayenne pepper
1 pt. sour cream, room temperature
2 T. Dijon mustard
1/2 stick butter
1 heaping T. prepared horseradish
6 green onions, chopped

In a kettle of water, place potatoes, crab boil, salt, and cayenne pepper and boil until done. Chop potatoes in a baking dish. Add remaining ingredients and blend together well. A real treat!

Serves 6-8

ROSEMARY AND GARLIC SWEET POTATOES

4 lbs. sweet potatoes
1/2 C. olive oil
1 1/2 T. dried rosemary, crumbled
24 unpeeled garlic cloves, flattened
freshly ground pepper to taste

Peel and cut sweet potatoes into 1/3 to 1/2-inch thick rounds. Combine with other ingredients (season generously with pepper) and divide mixture into two large baking dishes (or disposable aluminum pans). Stir to coat sweet potatoes. Grill over medium fire (or bake in a 450-degree oven) about 50 minutes or until potatoes are tender and crusty. Stir occasionally while cooking. Remove garlic before serving.

Serves 12

CUSTER'S EOLA HOTEL PICKLED VIDALIA ONIONS

3 Vidalia onions

MARINADE:

1/4 C. minced white onion
1 C. vegetable oil
1/2 C. sugar
1/2 C. white vinegar
1 t. dry mustard
1/2 t. red pepper
salt to taste

Prepare the marinade and add peeled and sliced onions, separated into rings (be sure you have enough liquid to cover the onions). Let marinate 12 to 24 hours. Serve as a side dish with any barbecue. Make more than you think you'll need—they're eaten quickly and you'll wish you had more!

Serves 6-8

RAZORBACK BARBEQUED ONIONS

6 medium onions
1-2 sticks butter
salt and pepper to taste
Razorback Barbeque Sauce (hot or mild)

Peel onions and remove centers. Fill with butter, salt, and pepper to taste. Place each onion on a square of aluminum foil and cover with sauce. Twist top of foil tightly and place over medium-hot fire for 1 to 2 hours or in a 300-degree oven for about 1 hour.

Serves 6

W'HAM STIRS

1 T. pork fat, shortening, or vegetable oil
6 C. white cabbage, shredded
1/4 C. red cabbage, shredded
1/2 C. onion, halved and sliced
1/2 C. yellow squash, sliced
1/4 C. red bell pepper, sliced
1/4 C. cauliflower florets
1/4 C. sprouts
1/4 C. W'ham marinade (from directions on seasoning bottle)

In a large pan, heat fat to boiling, then add cabbage, onion, and squash. Stir and allow to come to a simmer. Stir 2 minutes more, then add pepper, cauliflower, bean sprouts, and W'ham sauce. When mixture reaches simmer again, allow to cook for 3 minutes, stirring continuously. Remove from heat and serve.

Variation: Pork, turkey ham, diced chicken, or bacon may be added to make a one-dish meal. Allow meat to warm and brown in fat, then add vegetables and marinade as directed above.

Serves 6-8

HAWG'S BEST BAR-B-QUE CABBAGE

1 large head of cabbage
1 stick butter or margarine
2 T. Bull's Eye Bar-B-Que Sauce
salt and pepper to taste

Cut cabbage into 6 or 8 wedges (leave outer leaves on). Melt butter and mix with barbecue sauce. Spoon on sides of cabbage. Sprinkle lightly with salt and pepper. Wrap in foil and cook on grill (use indirect heat) until done to taste.

Serves 6-8

JOAN'S GARLIC CHEESE GRITS

1 C. grits
3 C. water
1 roll Kraft garlic cheese
1/4 C. margarine
2 eggs, well beaten
1/4 C. milk
red pepper, to taste
salt and pepper to taste
1/2 C. grated sharp cheese
paprika

Preheat oven to 300 degrees. Cook grits in water according to directions on package. To grits add garlic cheese, margarine, eggs, milk, red pepper, salt and pepper. Pour in a greased baking dish and bake for 45 minutes. Remove from oven and sprinkle with sharp cheese and paprika. Return to oven and bake 15 minutes longer.

Serves 6-8

GRILLED CORN ON THE COB

fresh yellow or white corn in husks (1-2 ears per person)
butter
salt and pepper

Pull husks down (3 or 4 inches) and remove corn silks. Soak corn in iced water for 30 to 45 minutes. Replace husks and place ears on grill. Cook for about 45 minutes or until done. Remove from grill. Husks may be peeled back to form a "handle" or discarded. Butter and sprinkle with salt and pepper to taste.

KITTY'S FRIED OKRA

1 lb. fresh okra
salted ice water
vegetable oil
yellow cornmeal
salt and pepper, to taste
1 egg, beaten

Wash okra and slice into 1/2-inch pieces. Soak in salted ice water at least 15 minutes; remove from water and drain. (Frozen cut okra may be substituted for fresh; eliminate salted ice water soaking process.) Pour oil 1-inch deep into iron skillet, and heat to hot. Mix cornmeal, salt, and pepper. Drop okra into beaten egg, then coat in cornmeal mixture, a few slices at a time. Drop into hot oil and fry until okra is golden brown and floats to the surface. Remove from skillet and drain on paper towels.

Serves 4-6

DEE'S CROOKED NECK SQUASH

4 medium yellow crooked neck squash, sliced
salt and pepper to taste

Layer sliced squash on heavy-duty aluminum foil, sprinkle salt and pepper between layers. Tightly close foil and place in disposable aluminum pan. Cook over medium hot fire for 20 to 30 minutes.

Serves 6-8

DESSERTS

DONNA'S CORN PUDDING

2 T. cold water
2 T. cornstarch
2 (No. 2) cans cream-style corn
2 T. sugar
2 T. salt
3/4 stick butter, melted
10 eggs, well beaten
1 1/2 pt. milk

Dissolve cornstarch in water and mix with all other ingredients. Pour into a greased 4-quart casserole dish; cover and bake at 350 degrees for about 1 hour until custard is firm. This also can be cooked on a closed grill.

Serves 12 or more

JESSICA'S MISSISSIPPI MUD

1 (8 oz.) pkg. cream cheese, softened
1 stick butter, softened
1 C. sugar
3 C. milk
2 pkgs. instant vanilla pudding
1 1/2 t. vanilla
1 (12 oz.) carton of non-dairy whipped topping
1 large pkg. Hydrox cookies, crushed

Cream together cream cheese, butter, and sugar. Add milk, pudding, vanilla, and non-dairy topping; mix until well blended. Place half the crushed cookies in the bottoms of two 8 x 11-inch glass casseroles. Pour cream mixture over cookie crumbs and top with remaining cookies. Freeze overnight.

Serves 24-30

SHERYL'S CHOCOLATE BROWNIE PIE

1 square chocolate
2 T. butter
3 large eggs
1/2 C. sugar
3/4 C. dark corn syrup
3/4 C. pecan halves

Melt together chocolate and butter in double boiler. Beat together the eggs, sugar, chocolate mixture, and syrup. Stir in pecan halves. Pour into a 9-inch un-baked pie shell. Bake 15 minutes at 400 degrees, then 30 minutes at 350 degrees or until set. Serve with ice cream or whipped cream.

Serves 6-8

PIG DIAMONDS PECAN COOKIES

1 C. self-rising flour
1 C. brown sugar
3/4 t. salt
1 egg, beaten
1 t. vanilla
1/3 C. shortening
1/2 C. chopped pecans

Mix the first three ingredients, then add egg and vanilla. Add shortening, mix well, and then add nuts. Dough will be stiff. Drop by teaspoonfuls onto greased cookie sheets. Bake at 350 degrees for 8 to 10 minutes. Broil for a minute to brown the tops.

Makes 3 dozen

PADDLEWHEEL PORKERS
"THE JUDGE IS A COMIN' . . ."

2 eggs
3/4 C. crumbled vanilla wafers
3/4 C. butter
2 squares unsweetened chocolate
2 C. powdered sugar

1 C. chopped pecans
1 T. vanilla
ice cream, softened
pecan halves, cherries for garnish

Separate eggs. Beat yolks slightly; beat whites until stiff. Place crumbs in a 9 x 13 x 2-inch baking pan. In a saucepan, melt butter and chocolate. Add sugar, chopped pecans, and vanilla. When blended, remove from heat and fold in egg whites. Pour mixture over crumbs. Chill until firm. Cover pan with softened ice cream and freeze. Before serving, garnish with pecan halves and/or cherries.

Serves 10-12

"SPENCE SPECIAL"

1 (46 oz.) can red Hawaiian Punch
1 large can crushed pineapple
    and its juice
2 (13 oz.) cans evaporated milk
2 (6 oz.) cans orange juice concentrate

3 whole eggs
juice of 3 lemons
2 1/2 C. sugar, dissolved in
    Hawaiian Punch
1 C. light corn syrup

Put ice and salt in an ice cream freezer; combine ingredients in the freezer container. Crank until the mixture is frozen (it will have the consistency of a frosty sherbet).

This delicious concoction, inspired by a hot summer day, a new electric ice cream freezer, and an active imagination, was created by C. C. "Buster" Spence in 1948. The Holy Smokers, Too serve this favorite to judges at the barbecue competitions to cleanse their palates.

Serves 10-15

MATT'S BREAD PUDDING WITH WHISKEY SAUCE

3 large eggs
1 C. sugar
2 C. milk
1 t. vanilla
1/2 t. nutmeg
1/2 t. cinnamon
pinch of salt
1/2 C. raisins
1/2 C. chopped dry roasted pecans
6 C. stale Italian bread, cubed
butter

WHISKEY SAUCE:

1 1/4 C. water
1/2 C. light brown sugar, firmly packed
1/4 C. Jack Daniels
1 1/2 T. cornstarch
2 T. butter

Preheat oven to 375 degrees. Beat eggs until frothy; beat in sugar. Add milk, vanilla, nutmeg, cinnamon, and salt; stir to mix. Add raisins and pecans, then pour mixture over bread crumbs. Toss together and let soak until a small bead of liquid is on the side of the bowl. Pour bread mixture into a generously buttered 1 1/2-quart casserole. dish. Bake for 40 minutes or until a toothpick comes out clean.

To make whiskey sauce, combine water and sugar in a saucepan. Bring to a boil. Blend whiskey and cornstarch and stir into sugar mixture; cook until thick. Blend in the butter until melted.

Serve pudding warm topped with sauce.

Serves 6-8

RESTAURANTS

LEONARD'S

571 South Mendenhall (683-4813)
5465 Fox Plaza Drive (360-1963)
4560 Elvis Presley (396-7044)

Open daily for lunch and dinner
(dining in, carry out, catering, banquets)

Leonard's fame began in the early days of Memphis barbecue with Leonard Heuberger and his famous "pig sandwich" (a tasty mating of shredded pork and sauce topped with slaw and served on a bun). Leonard's can boast longevity with their personable pit cook, James Willis, who has been cooking for over 50 years and was recently included as one of the great barbecue personalities on the PBS "Great Chefs-Great Barbecue" show. *Memphis* magazine adds to their fame as one of the "1988 Great Eight." But the real test is the palate. The menu includes the staples (ribs and pork shoulder) with your choice of onion rings, fries, slaw, skillet apples, barbecue beans, salad, and potato salad. They have great "pig sandwiches" and an offering of catfish, chicken, and spaghetti. But, please save room for their homemade lemon icebox pie!

GERMANTOWN COMMISSARY

2290 Germantown Road South
754-5540

Open daily for lunch and dinner
(dining in, carry out)

This barbecue hamlet was formerly a family-owned grocery store, serving barbecue for carry out only. It still has that homey feel with its barnwood walls and sports memorabilia, rustic and quaint. Owner Walker Taylor is there to greet his hungry customers. He says that you can carry out just about everything except his "barbecue pork nachos." In addition to the ribs and pork shoulder, he offers barbecue shrimp, burgers, and chicken. All the fixings for a picnic are here: beans, cole slaw, potato salad, deviled eggs, homemade pies, and cheesecakes (including picnic tables around the side of the building). Don't forget to try their "pig sandwich," which was ranked by *Memphis* magazine as one of the best.

THE PUBLIC EYE

17 South Cooper (Overton Square) 726-4040
111 Court Avenue (Downtown) 527-5757
Mall of Memphis Food Court

Open daily for lunch and dinner at Overton Square; Monday-Saturday for lunch and dinner downtown (closed Sunday)
(dining in, carry out, catering, banquets)

The atmosphere here is fun. You know that as soon as you see the sign that says "Swine Dining." Fresh popcorn from an old-fashioned popper greets you as you enter this friendly, casual place. There's plenty of room in the ample-sized bar if you have to wait (while you salivate). Ribs, shredded pork, and shredded beef sandwiches are complemented with corn on the cob and slaw. Public Eye serves chili, soups, sandwiches, and sinful desserts: fudge pie, pecan pie, and apple streusel pie. Owner David Sorin says that "Public Eye barbecue has appeared then disappeared" when served to such notables as the National Press Club. His long distance carry out has reached the likes of Larry Gatlin, Senator Jim Sasser, and ZZ Top. His best story is that he's listed in a French guide book, *A Student's Guide to the USA,* and several French students haave found their way to the Public Eye. This is one of the "1988 Great Eight" restaurants selected by *Memphis* magazine.

INTERSTATE BAR-B-Q & RESTAURANT

2265 South Third
775-2304

Open daily for lunch and dinner
(dining in, carry out)

The majority of Memphis barbecue restaurants are located from downtown to the east, so Jim Neely's Interstate Bar-B-Q received a warm southwest neighborhood welcome when he opened his doors. He serves a wide variety of barbecue in an old-fashioned friendly atmosphere. Your choices include the traditional pork shoulder and pork ribs, plus barbecue beef sandwiches and beef ribs. Several sausages are offered, along with beans, slaw, and barbecue spaghetti. Try a nice cool ice cream cone to finish the meal or take some hand-packed ice cream home with you. The carry-out area is separate from the dine-in area, with plenty of room for a big crowd. The Neelys are very accommodating and efficient, so you don't wait long to take that carry out home. If you eat in, the service is the same. The atmosphere is clean and uncluttered with wood-paneled walls and formica-topped tables, neat and simple. Jim has his sights on some other locations, too, which would still be family affairs with his sons and nephews heading the operations.

RENDEZVOUS

52 South Second Street
523-2746

Open Friday and Saturday for lunch and dinner; open Tuesday-Saturday for dinner (closed Sunday and Monday)
(dining in, carry out, banquets Tuesday-Thursday)

This is the place for Memphis's famous "dry ribs." Charlie Vergos and his sons run what many call the epitome of a barbecue restaurant. In this eclectic downstairs tavern/cavern-style eatery, one winds through several interconnecting rooms of all sizes. The warm wood and brick structure is adorned with memorabilia everywhere, with hardly an inch of bare wall showing. It's a wonderful place for browsing. And a "1988 Great Eight" place for dining. The fare starts with a relish tray of smoked sausage, pickles, and cheese. Choose your entree from the famous ribs, pork loin, chicken, or lamb riblets. With a 24-hour notice you can reserve a skillet of barbecue shrimp. The Vergos family has been serving barbecue for over a quarter of a century in this 10,000-square-foot cellar. They've been expressing their ribs and pork shoulder all over the country for the last few years and look forward to their phone orders from Bill Cosby a couple of times a year.

THE BAR-B-Q SHOP
1782 Madison Avenue
272-1277

Open daily for lunch and dinner
(dining in, carry out, catering)

This charming place used to be the Black Eyed Pea. It has a high molded tin ceiling, rust-colored walls, and attractive wooden bench booths. The bar is a showpiece. The beautifully carved wooden backdrop with mirrored arches used to be a five-unit Catholic confessional. The belly-up-to-the-bar part has old newspaper clippings and magazine articles spread the entire length. A large brick oven is part of the back wall in the dining area . . . and this is where it all happens. Owner Frank Vernon has been serving up great barbecue for years. His menu includes barbecue beans or barbecue spaghetti, slaw, and hot bread with his barbecue pork shoulder, beef brisket, or chicken breast. For the hungry man, there's a "Bar-B-Q Shop Special"—ribs, Boston butt shoulder, beef brisket, barbecue spaghetti, and barbecue beans. His hot chicken drummies with bleu cheese are a winner, too. Frank is a confident and friendly man, which is reflected in his uptown shop. He knows his barbecue and can be found judging at the "big one," Memphis in May.

GRIDLEY'S
4101 Summer 346-2260   6065 Macon 388-7003
5339 Elvis Presley 452-4057   6430 Winchester 794-5997

Open daily for lunch and dinner
(dining in, carry out, catering, banquets)

The atmosphere here is very simple and plain, with each of the four locations having a "chain" look. But the food samplings are real good. Specials are served with beans, slaw, and a loaf of Gridley's hot baked bread. You have your choice of chicken, shrimp, beef, pork, and, of course, ribs. Try the Blues-B-Q salad, piled high with either shredded beef brisket or pork shoulder. Whatever you get, it will be a feast for your eyes and your stomach. The Gridley family owns the four Memphis locations and have franchised another unit in Jackson, Mississippi. They also do their share of shipping ribs and sauce to each of the fifty states and even some foreign countries. With Federal Express headquarters in Memphis, it's no wonder that Memphis is the "capital of Federal Expressed ribs."

CORKY'S

5259 Poplar Avenue
685-9744

Open daily for lunch and dinner
(dining in, carry out, catering)

This is one of the newest barbecue restaurants on the scene and is already gaining fame as one of the "1988 Great Eight" from *Memphis* magazine. Corky's is a charmer with a cozy atmosphere (seats 68). Museum art posters of old model cars are hung everywhere, barnwood stretches across the walls and ceiling, there's lots of brass accents throughout, and they play classic '50s and '60s music . . . all adding up to a great place. But the food is the tops, with wet or dry ribs, pork shoulder piled high on your plate, and wonderful home-baked bread. Fudge pie for dessert is to die for (if you have room, because you need to try the great onion rings that come stacked on a plate). Owner Don Pelts has made it real easy to carry out—just pull up to the drive-in window. What a wonderful aroma to drive home with!

PAYNE'S

1762 Lamar Avenue
272-1523

Open for lunch Monday-Saturday (closed Sunday); open for dinner daily except Wednesday and Sunday

(dining in, carry out)

This barbecue hideaway was highly recommended by Greg Johnson and Vince Staten, authors of *Real Barbecue*. These guys know their stuff and traveled all over the country to find "the best joints, the best sauces, the best cookers and much more." They rated Payne's "as good as we've ever had." This is true. Emily Payne and her daughter-in-law Flora serve a mean pork shoulder in the traditional Memphis "pig sandwich" style. They pile the meat high without need of a scale to weigh portions. Their rib sandwich has a tangy mustard relish; it's a must and you'll go back for more. The place is as plain as they come—it was converted from a filling station and seats just about forty people. Get there early for lunch or go a little late or you may have to wait, but the wait is definitely worth it!

JOHN WILLS PIT BBQ

5101 Sanderlin
761-5101

Open daily for lunch and dinner
(dining in, carry out, catering)

John Wills is a true success story of a Memphis in May competitor turned pro! And pro he is, rating among the *Memphis* magazine's "1988 Great Eight." His competitive years earned him Grand Champion twice. A restauranteur since 1983, John runs one of the most popular places in town. His pork sandwich is tops, along with his barbecued beef brisket and ribs. Other choices are beef ribs, sausage, barbecued spaghetti, slaw, and spicy slow-cooked beans. John says his barbecued bologna is popular "not because it's cheap, but because it tastes good." His place feels like a barbecue place should. There's lots of wood, '60s music, bustling in the kitchen—and great hog pictures on the walls! Once there, you'll go back for more . . . just what John Wills is counting on.

MAIL ORDER

As a result of their successes in barbecue cooking competitions, many of the teams listed in *Barbecue Greats—Memphis Style* have begun marketing barbecue-related products. Those products are listed here as a reader service. Write or call for particulars and to order.

J-R ENTERPRISES. Jerry Roach designed his first barbecue pit in 1979. In 1983, he entered his first barbecue competition as J-R's Cook'n'Crew. He has won over a hundred awards, including the 1986 Memphis in May International Barbecue Team of the Year. His cooker worked so well that fellow competitors commissioned him to make cookers for them and a new industry was born. J-R Enterprises custom designs and builds commercial, residential, and contest cookers and accessories. If you purchase one of his cookers, Jerry will also share his secrets of barbecue success with you. For information and brochure, write: Jerry Roach, J-R Enterprises, Route 1, Box 249A, DeWitt, AR 72042, or call (501) 946-2780 (out of state, (800) 432-8187).

JIM QUESSENBERRY'S "SAUCE BEAUTIFUL". This secret blend has been used by Mr. Q and his Arkansas Trav'lers team to win more prizes than we have room to list here. For prices, sizes, etc., write: Arkansas Trav'ler Jim Quessenberry, 206 E. Merriman, Wynne, AR 72396. Wholesale inquiries welcome.

CATFISH LIL'S BBQ MARINADE is the perfect complement to the pond-raised catfish she promotes. This barbecue spice can be mixed with water and used as a marinade or applied dry before grilling. It works on other types of fish as well as catfish. Catfish Lil sells her spice in 3.2 oz. or 16 oz. bottles, or, when you really get hooked, in 5 lb. buckets. Write Catfish Lil, Route 1, Box 150, Tunica, MS 38676, or call (601) 363-2688. She accepts payment by cash, check, or money order.

WILLINGHAMS. In 1971, John Willingham began his search for the best available method for cooking barbecue. Not satisfied with what he found, he developed his own "W'ham Turbo Cooker." Naturally, he next developed a line of seasonings and spices to further enhance barbecue cooking. With a complete "package," John decided to put his cooking method, seasoning, and sauce to the test in the 1983 Memphis in May Contest. He won the Grand Championship that year and then again in 1984. John sells his W'ham cookers, sauces, seasonings, and barbecue meats (Rib Rac Pacs and "Karanuf" pacs) by mail and Federal

Express. He accepts cash, check, and most major credit cards. Write: John Willingham, Willingham's World Champion BBQ, 6189 Heather Dr., Memphis, TN 38119, or call (901) 362-RIBS.

CAJUN COUNTRY SEASONING is the barbecue spice used so successfully by the Cajun Country Cookers, the 1987 Memphis in May Grand Champion team. This family recipe, passed along to Darrell Hicks by his father, is a delicious blend of Cajun spices that enhances most barbecued foods. Cajun Country Cookers also markets Cajun Country Rice. Write: Cajun Country Cookers, P.O. Box 3201, Jackson, TN 38303.

RAZORBACK is the fitting brand name for Ray "Red" Gill's line of dry, liquid, and basting barbecue sauces. His River City Spice company has been manufacturing his unique blends since 1983 in the plant near Blytheville, Arkansas. The Razorback Cookers have won five State Championships, including in their native Arkansas. Red's ribs were voted "World's Best Baby-Back Ribs" in Richmond, Virgina, in 1988. Razorback products are available by writing: Ray "Red" Gill, P.O. Box 631, Blytheville, AR 72315, or call (501) 763-7950.

WICKER BARBECUE PRODUCTS is not a team profiled in this book. But several of the teams represented in *Barbecue Greats* use it, and it's sometimes hard to find. Wicker's BBQ Marinade and Baste is a blend of vinegar and spices that enhances most barbecue meats. It was voted "Best Baste in America" twice at the National Barbecue Sauce Tasting Contest. Also available are Wicker's Thicker (table sauce) and Low Sodium varieties. They sell some "exotic" wood chips (apple, cherry, hickory, mesquite, sassafras, and grapevine). Write: Wicker Barbecue Products, P.O. Box 126, Hornersville, MO 63855, or call (800) 847-0032 (in Missouri, (314) 737-2372).

RENDEZVOUS. Charlie Vergos has been dubbed the "Dean of the Dry School" by Greg Johnson and Vince Staten in *Real Barbecue*. He smokes his ribs without seasoning and tops them with Rendezvous Seasoning before serving. The Rendezvous has been a favorite Memphis eatery since 1948, and now ships ribs, sauce, and Mr. Charlie's famous seasoning by mail and Federal Express. Write: The Rendezvous, 52 South Second St., Memphis, TN 38103, or call (901) 523-2746.

GRIDLEY'S has served up Memphis-style barbecue since 1975. Clyde Gridley has perfected his own "secret" sauce and his ribs have consistently rated well in reader polls in the *Commercial Appeal* and *Memphis* magazine. Gridley's ships pork or ribs and sauce by Federal Express. Call (800) 222-RIBS, or in Tennessee (901) 794-5997.

THOMASON SEASONINGS was formed as a result of winning many barbecue contests with the Tail Twisters's unique "Shake Sauce." This spice blend seals the meat, and its delicious flavor permeates throughout. Write: Thomason Seasonings, P.O. Box 523, Kennett, MO 63857.

CORKY'S is one of the most recent additions to the barbecue restaurants of Memphis and have jumped right into overnight delivery of their ribs, pork shoulder, and Corky's sauce. You can also order a Corky's T-shirt or a Corky's apron. Write: Corky's Bar-B-Q, 5259 Poplar Ave., Memphis, TN 38119 or call (800) 284-RIBS.

PUBLIC EYE will offer its "Swine Dining" to anyone in the country by Federal Express. To order your ribs, write: Public Eye, 17 South Cooper, Memphis, TN 38104, or call (901) 726-4040.

GERMANTOWN COMMISSARY will Federal Express their "Epicurean BBQ Pork Shoulder and Ribs" if you call (901) 754-5540. Too bad you can't have them ship their barbecue pork nachos, too; guess you'll have to put them on your places to visit.

JOHN WILLS PIT BBQ. You can't get John's barbecue bologna, but he'll Federal Express just about everything else. To order, call (901) 761-5101.

Several companies specialize in gift packages of Memphis products and barbecue products in particular. Write or call for descriptions or catalogs of their offerings:

A BASKET CASE
966 Poplar Avenue
Memphis, TN 38117
(901) 683-1700

HUNTER BASQUETRIE, INC.
376 Perkins Extended
Memphis, TN 38117
(901) 386-1988

DELECTABLES LTD.
4741 Poplar Avenue
Memphis, TN 38117
(901) 767-1987

METRO MARKETING
6554 Winchester Road, #149
Memphis, TN 38115
(816) 763-8823

GIFT BASKETS GALORE
1432 Union Avenue
Memphis, TN 38104
(901) 726-9101

PEABODY GIFTSHOP
149 Union
Memphis, TN 38103
(901) 526-3825

BOOKS ON BARBECUE

A saucy sampling of additional reading pleasure!

BARBEQUE: SIZZLING FIRESIDE KNOW-HOW by Leslie Bloom (1987, American Cooking Guild)

COMPANY'S COMING BARBECUES by Jean Paré (1991, Company's Coming Publishing Limited)

GREAT AMERICAN BARBEQUE by "Smoky" Hale (1989, Abacus Publishing Company)

GRILL LOVERS COOKBOOK (1985, from Char-Broil, Columbus, GA)

JACK DANIEL'S OLD TIME BARBECUE COOKBOOK by Vince Staten (1991, Jack Daniel Distillery, Lem Motlow Prop.)

THE JOY OF GRILLING by Joe Famularo (1988, Barron's)

KANSAS CITY BBQ—THE HOW TO & WHERE TO OF KANSAS CITY BARBECUE by Bill Venable and Rick Welch (1989, Pig Out Publications)

MEMPHIS BARBECUE, BARBEQUE, BAR-B-Q, B-B-Q by Carolyn Wells (1991, Pig Out Publications)

THE PASSION OF BARBEQUE by the Kansas City Barbeque Society (1988, Pig Out Publications)

THE THRILL OF THE GRILL by Chris Schlesinger & John Willoughby (1990, William Morrow and Company, Inc.)

ABOUT THE AUTHOR

Carolyn Wells is hog wild for barbecue. She cut her teeth on rib bones and blossomed on plenty of backyard barbecue, church "socials," and pig sandwiches from barbecue joints in her native Nashville.

By adulthood she definitely had basting sauce in her veins. She even pursued a career in 'que. For thirteen years she was affiliated with Wicker Barbecue Products Company in Hornersville, Missouri (about 80 miles from Memphis). Through this association, she became acquainted with (and addicted to) Memphis-style barbecue, sampling it at the great Memphis barbecue restaurants and at the barbecue contests she attended. She even began entering the contests herself and to date has won over fifty trophies and ribbons in various competitions. In 1987, she left Wicker's and started a barbecue-related marketing and consulting business.

Carolyn lives now with her husband Gary and family in the Kansas City area. Among her current pursuits, she is an owner and partner in Pig Out Publications and author of Memphis Barbecue, Barbeque, Bar-B-Q, B-B-Q.